ONE MINUTE
OF YOUR
Day

Carol ❤
May these "thoughts"
start your day the right way
each morning!
Merry Christmas
Love, Anne

ONE MINUTE
OF YOUR
Day

BRYANT WRIGHT

WINEPRESS WP PUBLISHING

WinePress Publishing (PO Box 428, Enumclaw, WA 98022) functions only as book publisher. As such, the ultimate design, content, editorial accuracy, and views expressed or implied in this work are those of the author.

Cover designed and printed by Winepress Publishing in the United States of America.

Unless otherwise noted, all Scriptures are taken from the Holy Bible, New American Standard Version, Copyright 1960, 1962, 1963, 1968, 1971, 1972, 1973, 1975, 1977, 1995 by the Lockman Foundation. Used by permission.

Scripture references marked NIV are taken from the New International Bible, Copyright 1973, 1978, 1984 by the International Bible Society. Used by permission of Zondervan Publishing House. The "NIV" and "New International Version" trademarks are registered in the United States Patent and Trademark Office by International Bible Society.

Scripture references marked KJV are taken from the King James Version of the Bible.

ISBN 1-57921-841-5
Library of Congress Catalog Card Number: 2006900375

So will My word be which goes forth from My mouth; it will not return to Me empty without accomplishing what I desire, and without succeeding in the matter for which I sent it.
—Isaiah 55:11

DEDICATIONS

This book is dedicated to George and Beth Wright, my loving and supportive Christian parents, whose wisdom flows through these pages, and to Bob and Marge Hoskins for raising a wonderful Christian daughter, my wife Anne, who blesses my life daily.

ACKNOWLEDGEMENTS

Jerry Maxfield, for without his leadership this book would not be possible.

Olivia Mahon, as my executive assistant, helped type these thoughts; most of all, she helps keep my life organized.

Tracy Loescher, Stephanie Buice, and Cheryl Erickson for typing spots; Krista Henson for proofing spots; Deborah Riddle, Mary Stephens, and Charlie Strickland for organizing and producing these spots for radio and television. Jennifer Schuchmann and Teisha Moseley for editorial refinement.

The Right From The Heart board and staff—a much-appreciated team for support, encouragement, and wise counsel.

Johnson Ferry Baptist Church, for almost all these thoughts came from nuggets of sermons preached there.

Anne Wright, my devoted wife and best friend, whose insight is invaluable.

January 1

LASTING CHANGE

"Therefore if anyone is in Christ, he is a new creature; the old things have passed away, behold, new things have come!"
—2 Corinthians 5:17

Ahh—another new year. The old one has gone. The new one has come, ready or not. Most of us will admit we have character traits or habits we would like to change. Some of us even try to modify our behavior. But just changing outward behavior is like rolling back the odometer on a car. You reduce the numbers from 200,000 to 20,000, but you still have a car with 200,000 miles on it.

However, there is hope for the person who sincerely desires to change. The power to change like that means admitting we can't do it on our own. Remember, lasting change comes from within. We need the help of the Lord.

The Bible says if anyone is in Christ, he is a new creation; the old is gone and new has come. When we give our lives to Jesus Christ, He transforms us—changes us from the inside out. Instead of just rolling back the odometer and being the same old person inside, He gives us a spiritual heart transplant.

Now, that's a change for the better. And a change that lasts.

Getting Off to a Good Start in the Morning

"In the morning, O LORD, You will hear my voice; In the morning I will order my prayer to You and eagerly watch."
—Psalm 5:3

Are you a morning person or a night person? Because of commitments to work and school, my wife and I have to be up and going in the morning, but millions of people don't get going until about three o'clock in the afternoon. That's when their creative juices start flowing and when they really feel alive. For most of us, the day begins much earlier.

Even if you're a night owl, let me suggest a great way to start your day. The writer of Psalms knew the key: "In the morning, O Lord, You will hear my voice (or prayer)."

Doesn't it make sense to be in touch with the One who created the day? Why not begin your day by spending a few minutes alone with God each morning? Study God's Word and share with Him through prayer your heart and your concerns. It will help get you in the right frame of mind. You'll find your day will start and finish a whole lot better.

Purpose for Living

"He who has the Son has the life; he who does not have the Son of God does not have the life."
—1 John 5:12

What is your purpose for living? Have you ever taken time to pause in the rat race of life and figure out why you're in it?

I recommend developing a life-purpose statement. A man once told me his purpose statement was to "Get all you can; can all you get; and sit on the can!" I hope that when you develop your purpose statement, it'll be more than that.

Don't be shortsighted, focusing on this life alone. Keep eternity in mind. God created all of us for a purpose. What's yours?

Here's a hint. Knowing God has put you on this earth for a purpose becomes clear when you get to know the person of Jesus Christ. With Him, it's amazing how all things become clear. Otherwise, you end up like the masses, too busy to take time to know why you're here and too lost to know where you're going.

Are you racing through life going nowhere fast?

Stop for a second. Look to God in Christ and discover the purpose of your life.

FRIENDS

"A friend loves at all times . . ."
—Proverbs 17:17

What is your definition of true friendship?

Ralph Waldo Emerson said, "Happy is the house that shelters a friend," and "A friend is a person with whom I may be sincere and before him I may think aloud. The only reward of virtue is virtue; the only way to have a friend is to be one."

Walter Winchell defines a friend as "one who walks in when others walk out."

Someone else has said a friend is "a man who laughs at your funny stories, even when they ain't so good, and sympathizes with your misfortunes, even when they ain't so bad."

Do you have a friend?

Do you know true friendship?

Many, I'm sad to say, have to answer no. The good news is this: you can have a best friend forever. That friend is Jesus Christ. I encourage you to get to know Him. You'll never be disappointed. He'll always be there with you.

January 5

USE IT OR LOSE IT

". . . [Scripture gives] you the wisdom that leads to salvation
through faith which is in Christ Jesus."
—2 Timothy 3:15

I have friends who are learning to speak Spanish. They are struggling with different sounds, different sentence structures, and different words. Acquiring a new skill takes practice and patience. You have heard the cliché, "Use it or lose it." My friends realize that they have to use the few Spanish words they know or they will quickly forget them. We must use what we know, or we don't retain knowledge.

This principle applies in the spiritual dimension as well. Faith in God is like a muscle. The more you use it, the stronger it becomes. The manual for getting this muscle in shape is the Bible, and the personal trainer is Jesus Christ. If you submit yourself to His leadership and His guidance, you will discover how to use the faith muscle every day. It's either use it or lose it.

January 6

SEX IN MARRIAGE

*"Marriage is to be held in honor among all, and the marriage
bed is to be undefiled; for fornicators and adulterers
God will judge."*
—Hebrews 13:4

How's your sex life?

Have you bought into the idea that the best, most enjoyable, most intense sex is always found outside of marriage? We are constantly bombarded with this message by TV, movies, books, and songs.

This message is a lie. It is the opposite of what God had in mind when He invented sex. Any sex outside the context of committed love in marriage is always less than the best. It brings emotional harm, broken relationships, turmoil, and guilt. That might sell movies and books, but in the end it destroys a person's life. God intended sexual intimacy to be His great gift for marriage and marriage alone. He knows how it is best enjoyed.

Seek to trust the inventor of sex to experience the sacred enjoyment God has in mind for you. Quit settling for second best. Seek God's best for the best sex.

LYING

"Deliver my soul, O LORD, from lying lips,
[and] from a deceitful tongue."
—Psalm 120:2

An excited husband called to tell his wife he had been asked to accompany his boss on a fishing expedition to Canada. The husband had to leave that evening and asked his wife if she would mind packing a few things for him. He added, "Be sure to include my new silk pajamas."

She thought that sounded 'fishy', but said nothing. When the man returned from his trip. His wife asked how it went.

"Great," he said.

"Did you catch anything?" she asked.

"Yes, pike and walleye. What fun!" Then he asked, "But why didn't you pack my blue silk pajamas?"

"I did," she said. "They were in your tackle box."

Lying is, most of all, about stupidity. You will be found out. You may be getting away with it for now. But in the end, the truth comes out. It may not be until you die, but God has on file everything you've ever said. You'd be wise to seek His forgiveness and start telling the truth. Always! Otherwise, you'll eventually look like a stupid fool.

Financial Security

"Everything in the heavens and earth is yours, O Lord,
and this is your kingdom."
—1 Chronicles 29:11 (TLB)

There is a ton of financial insecurity today. When the economy is good, people worry it may go in the tank. When it's bad, pessimism reigns. All this adds up to a lot of financial insecurity, especially after the holidays when bills come due.

There is one key to financial security: understanding that God owns it all. That's not easy to do. For many, it is the toughest decision to make. That's why Jesus said you must choose where you're going to put your trust—in God, or in money.

Trusting in money in the form of a job, bank account, or investments, without God, always leads to worry, anxiety, and a spirit of greed or hoarding.

Trusting in God brings inner peace. His principles, as found in the Bible, teach us how to be good money managers. God promises to meet our needs. Not our wants, but our needs.

In these days of financial insecurity, find your security in God, not money. Understand He owns it all; seek to manage His money His way. It's the key to financial security.

BODILY ABUSE

*"It is not good to eat much honey, nor is it glory
to search out one's own glory."*
—Proverbs 25:27

Christianity teaches that the body is the temple of God's Spirit and that we are to take care of our bodies. But gluttony and obesity in America are at epidemic levels. And primarily among teenage girls and young women, the sin of gluttony can result in the opposite extreme, an eating disorder.

The original intent of those who suffer from eating disorders was to take care of their bodies by eating less. But over time they can become obsessed by controlling their food intake in a way that is similar to gluttony, but with the opposite effect.

There are three main types of eating disorders:

Anorexia—eating too little or being rigidly obsessed with avoiding perceived unhealthy foods.

Bulimia—binge eating and then throwing up or taking laxatives to avoid weight gain.

Exercise Bulimia—an obsession with exercise without enough caloric intake to replace the caloric output.

Each can bring great harm to the body. And like all addictions, whether food, booze, drugs, or sex, the addiction substitutes for the place of God in the addicted person's life. Anyone suffering from an addiction that harms the body, should seek God's forgiveness and His help. Others can then come alongside to help achieve victory over the unhealthy addiction.

January 10

Is Divorce OK?

*"Some Pharisees came up to Jesus, testing Him . . . whether it
was lawful for a man to divorce a wife."*
—**Mark 10:2**

People often ask me, "Can I get a divorce and still be right with God?"
Many want to know if divorce is ever OK.

Jesus was asked that question and He responded by talking about
marriage. The right question to ask is, "How can I make the most of
my marriage?"

Here's a hint. Several years ago Myron Augsberger did a survey that
found that even in a culture where one of every two marriages ends in
divorce, Christian marriages, where the couples are active in the church,
only end in divorce one out of every forty marriages. More amazing is the
fact that for Christian marriages where the couple has a daily devotional
life, there is only one divorce out of every four hundred marriages.

Going to church and being a Christian doesn't guarantee success
in marriage, but it sure helps the odds. And with one out of every two
marriages not making it, these are the odds I'm going to take. If you're
contemplating divorce and wondering if it is OK, why don't you ask
instead, "What can I do to make the most of my marriage?" With God's
help, you'll discover marriage as God intends it to be.

KEEP YOUR EYES ON THE GOAL

*"With all my heart I have sought You; do not let me wander
from your commandments."*
—Psalm 119:10

Walking through freshly fallen snow, a father wanted to teach his son a key lesson in life. He said, "Son, I'm going to walk to that tree fifty feet ahead in a perfectly straight line. Then I want you to do the same."

The father walked to the tree. He turned to look at his son and they both observed the perfectly straight tracks in the snow. Not wanting to fail the test, the son looked at his father and began to walk. He looked down at his steps and veered to the left. He looked up and corrected his course. He looked down again. He veered to the right and had to correct his course once more.

Arriving at the tree, his tracks told the story of his failure.

His father explained, "Son, as long as you focused on me, your tracks were straight. The moment you took your eyes off me, you got off track. The key is keeping your eyes on the goal."

So it is in life. There is one primary goal and if it becomes the heart and focus of your life, it will be the key to eternal success. That goal is following the Lord. Keep your eyes on Him, and He will keep you right on track to where you need to go.

APPOINTMENTS

*"Commit your works to the LORD
and your plans will be established."*
—Proverbs 16:3

Most of us have a pretty full plate, and that Palm Pilot or Day-Timer can fill up quickly. How do you keep your priorities in place?

Let me suggest three appointments you don't want to miss:

A regular daily appointment with God. Pick a time of the day to meet with God to communicate with Him through prayer and Bible study. When it comes to appointments, this one is the most important.

A weekly appointment in church. This is key if you claim to be a Christian, or have an openness to investigate Christianity. Remember, being in a church doesn't make you a Christian any more than being in a garage makes you a car, but it does help you stay close to God and get right with your fellow man.

A weekly date with your spouse, if you're married. You don't have to be a Christian to do this. The weekly date helps you stay close with your spouse all week long, and can rekindle those romantic fires.

These are three of life's most important appointments to keep on your calendar. Give 'em a try.

January 13

SELF-HELP

"Seek from the book of the LORD, and read . . ."
—Isaiah 34:16

Do you ever get tired of all the self-help information in society? There are books, radio programs, and numerous talk shows that urge you to take a look at who you are and then change yourself by your determined will.

Have you tried all that information and yet you're still discouraged by repeating the same old habits?

There are some things that self-help cannot help, things like disease, overcoming certain sins, and most of all, death.

But I have good news: God has a plan for us that goes beyond our abilities. It's something supernatural. It comes through a personal relationship with Jesus Christ, who supernaturally changes us where we can't change ourselves. As a bonus to that faith, He promises us victory over death, and eternal life. If you really want to help yourself, look beyond yourself to the only One who can save you and give you the ultimate victory—Jesus Christ.

January 14

KNOW PEACE IN WAR

"Fight the good fight of faith . . ."
—1 Timothy 6:12

William Tecumseh Sherman said, "War is hell."

A pastor friend said to me, "War is not hell. Hell is a place where certain people deserve to be, but war is a place where innocent women and children are killed. And they don't deserve that."

No doubt war is horrible. It is something no sane person wants. Yet many people are asking, "Is war ever right?"

Jesus teaches us to love our enemies and to seek to be peacemakers. Certainly, every Christian should. God's Word teaches that God has ordained government to administer justice, to defend and protect citizens, and to punish evil. How do we reconcile what seems to be contradictory teaching in God's Word? Jesus teaches us about the attitude of the individual and, later in God's Word, we learn about the role of government.

Let us pray for our government leaders and military personnel to protect and defend its citizens, to administer justice, and to punish evil effectively. Let us pray that when we have to go to war for a just cause, that we'll be blessed with victory and a minimal loss of life.

January 15

The Local Church and the Neighborhood Bar

". . . not forsaking our own assembling together, as is the habit
of some, but encouraging one another; and all the more
as you see the day drawing near."
—Hebrews 10:25

Have you ever thought of the similarities between the local church and the neighborhood bar? In both places:

- people come looking for fellowship;
- people want to go where others know their name;
- people want to go where they are accepted;
- people want to go where their spirits will be lifted;
- people are united around one theme;
- people go where they like the music.

Like a priest, the bartender serves by listening to people's troubles. But the differences are profound. The bar is centered on booze and the church is centered on Jesus Christ. The bar offers a way to escape problems. The church offers a way to face them, get through them, and overcome them. The spirit inside the bar lowers one's guard when it comes to temptation and sin. The spirit of the true church encourages people to turn from sin and turn to God.

The bar may be a substitute for the environment of the church, but it never comes close to providing the meaning and purpose found in a Christ-centered church.

January 16

FORGIVING OUR ENEMIES

"Be kind to one another, tender-hearted, forgiving each other,
just as God in Christ also has forgiven you."
—Ephesians 4:32

In 1962 in Montgomery, Alabama, a young, unknown Baptist preacher came home to find a large crowd gathered in front of his house that had just been bombed.

He ran inside to see if his wife and daughter had survived. He found they were unharmed. He comforted them before going outside to the large, angry crowd.

They had gathered with chains and weapons to retaliate against the white community for such a despicable deed. He told them there would be no retaliation saying, "Jesus tells us to love our enemies, to forgive those who persecute us. Now go home." Thus began the legacy of an amazing man with a unique spirit, Martin Luther King, Jr.

What King did on that occasion isn't natural—it's supernatural. The ability to forgive our enemies who have wronged us is often beyond our natural ability, but it is the Spirit of Christ. It is true Christianity. It is a power available to us all and it can change the world.

Tolerance and Diversity

*". . . walk in a manner worthy of the calling with which
you have been called, with all humility and gentleness, with
patience, showing tolerance for one another in love . . ."*
—Ephesians 4:1

Why is the tolerance and diversity movement so intolerant of biblical Christianity?

If tolerance is a supreme virtue of the politically correct, why is there such hypocrisy, such intolerance of Christian values?

If diversity is about openness and acceptance of all people, why do the diversity police seek to enforce their man-made rules on biblical Christianity?

Maybe it is because they don't understand the true definition of tolerance. Tolerance means accepting people even if you completely disagree with them, and not trying to force them to believe what you believe.

Christianity doesn't try to force anyone to believe in Jesus, but seeks to explain why it is a great way to live and believe. If you are really open-minded and tolerant, I hope you'll consider it. You'll find the church one of the most diverse groups in the world.

January 18

RIDDLED WITH GUILT

"Wash me thoroughly from my iniquity, and cleanse me from my sin. For I know my transgressions, and my sin is ever before me."
—Psalm 51:2–3

Are you riddled with guilt?

You need to be free from guilt, for it saps you physically, emotionally, and spiritually. When it comes to guilt, the best way to avoid it is simply to do what is right.

When you don't, you first need to confess your sin to God with a genuine desire to get things right. I promise that when you pursue the forgiveness of God through Jesus Christ, with an attitude of seeking to get things right, it will free you of guilt. He wipes the slate clean.

Second, seek forgiveness from those you have wronged. Make restitution.

Third, forgive yourself. Some struggle with this, but you should recognize that when God has forgiven you, you can forgive yourself.

Fourth, don't confuse forgiveness with the removal of consequences. God forgives immediately, but you have to deal with the consequences of your sin.

The good news is that you can be free of guilt when you seek to get things right—God's way.

DECEIT

"He is a shield to those who walk in integrity."
—Proverbs 2:7

In the movie *Liar, Liar,* Jim Carey starred as the profane attorney who was incapable of not lying for an entire day after his son made a birthday wish that his dad would stop lying.

Lying has become a pervasive problem. Have you fallen into the habit?

It seems that today's "me first" mindset places very little value on honesty and personal integrity. Truth is sacrificed on the altar of self-advancement. At the time, you may think that lying will make your life easier, but one lie almost always requires another and another and another. You have to remember everything you said to keep from confusing your lies.

But when you tell the truth, you don't have to remember what you said. That makes life a lot less complicated!

Which life have you created for yourself?

There's only one way to break the bondage of a lie, and that's with the truth. Seek to live with integrity and honesty and you'll find new freedom for living.

How? The truth is found in Jesus Christ. Find Him, and find the truth, the power, and strength to become a person of integrity.

January 20

KINDNESS

"But [a] fruit of the Spirit is . . . kindness."
—Galatians 5:22

Do you know one character trait that is always appreciated? Proverbs 19:22 tells us "What is desirable in a man is his kindness."

In the movie, *The Fugitive*, the character played by Harrison Ford performed several acts of kindness. The fugitive even risked his life to save the life of a boy who was being neglected in a busy emergency room. The cop, obsessed with chasing him, began to question whether this fugitive could have really killed his wife. You could just hear the cop thinking, "Cold-blooded killers don't do nice things like this."

Acts of kindness inspire us, whether it's taking time to help an employee at the office, or defending a person being picked on by bullies. The recipients of these acts of kindness are always grateful.

The one person who comes to mind when I think of kindness is Jesus Christ. He shows us that God is kind. And because He is so kind to us, we are to be kind to one another.

Especially in a busy world where so many seem to be looking out for number one, acts of kindness are always appreciated.

THE MOST DIFFICULT JOB

"Behold, children are a gift from the LORD . . ."
—Psalm 127:3

Have you ever considered what the most difficult job in life is? It's the job of parenting: the challenge of guiding a child through the demands of growing up and helping that child become all he or she was created to be.

The Bible provides timeless insight. "Train up a child in the way he should go, and when he is old he will not turn from it." The way he should go means according to his bent. This means we have to be students of our children—learning to recognize their God-given abilities and interests. We're also to help our children develop their strengths, as well as curb and check their weaknesses.

Once we become students of our children and teach them right from wrong with a lot of prayer, the promise of God can be realized. The challenge is a great one, but the rewards of seeing our children become mature, productive adults makes all the hard work worthwhile.

THE DAY AMERICA TOLD THE TRUTH

". . . every man did what was right in his own eyes."
—Judges 17:6

In the book, *The Day America Told the Truth*, Patterson and Kim found that in every region of the country, ninety percent of the people believe in God. But when they asked how they made up their mind on issues of right and wrong, they found people do not turn to God or religion to help them decide moral issues. They concluded, "There is absolutely no moral consensus at all."

In other words, people believe there is a God but He has no relevance to their everyday lives. True belief in God is about trust and obedience. We trust Him to know and want the best for us, so we obey His commands and His Word. It's radically counter-cultural, but it's the best way to live.

Having Jesus as Lord means loving God enough to trust and obey Him, and loving your neighbor as yourself. It connects God with morality in a way that is good for all.

What on Earth Am I Here For?

"Many plans are in a man's heart,
but the counsel of the LORD will stand."
—Proverbs 19:21

What on earth am I here for?

Have you ever asked yourself that question? Rick Warren asks that question in *The Purpose Driven Life*.

Are you clear on your life purpose? Can you write it down?

It seems the average American thinks life is all about working hard, raising a family, doing your best, making enough to retire (the earlier the better), and finally, doing what you want to do when you want to do it. But by mid-life, this philosophy makes a person cry, "What on earth am I here for?" It's like slowly drowning in an ocean of emptiness.

But I have good news. We can know what on earth we're here for. It begins when we get to know our Creator through the person of Christ. Our Creator, God, loves us and has a purpose for our lives. Our role is to trust Him and obey Him through His written word.

Don't waste your life. Get to know your Creator personally. I promise—you'll become clear about what on earth you're here for.

January 24

THE BUSIEST MAN WHO EVER LIVED

"Immediately Jesus made His disciples get into the boat and go ahead of Him to the other side to Bethsaida, while He Himself was sending the crowd away. After bidding them farewell, He left for the mountain to pray."
—**Mark 6:45–46**

He was exhausted, completely worn out from dealing with people and their problems. What He needed was a rest. He got away to spend some time alone with God. When He did, His spirit was renewed and refreshed. When the crowds came, He was able to respond, to care for them and meet their needs.

His name was Jesus Christ and He was the busiest man who ever lived. He accomplished more than anyone did before or since His time here.

We live in a fast-paced world with great demands on our time, yet no one has ever been busier than Jesus when He walked on this earth. Why not learn from Him when you're frazzled, exhausted, and burned out? Take some time to be with God. If Jesus needed time alone with God, surely we do as well.

OLD AGE AIN'T FOR SISSIES

". . . even to your graying years I will bear you! I have done it and I will carry you; and I will bear you and I will deliver you."
—Isaiah 46:4

Old age sure ain't for sissies. In Ecclesiastes, King Solomon agreed. He wrote of how the things we take for granted when we're young cause us to lose delight in living when we're old.

Our eyesight grows dim. We start with reading glasses and move to bifocals. Our hearing grows weak. We're constantly saying "Huh?" to our spouse. We have time to sleep late but we wake up early. Our hands start to tremble. Our desire for sex diminishes.

We become like the elderly man in the nursing home whose friends sent a beautiful young lady to his room for his birthday. She said, "Happy Birthday! I'm here to offer you super sex."

The old man paused and then said, "I believe I'll take the soup."

Old age isn't for sissies, and without God it can be meaningless. But with God, there is wisdom, strength, joy, and the hope that when the body finally gives out, there is life—real life—in heaven with God. It's something to remember when you're young and when you're old.

January 26

ORIGIN OF MARRIAGE

"But because of immoralities, each man is to have his own wife,
and each woman is to have her own husband."
—1 Corinthians 7:2

A hot topic in the news these days is marriage—or should we say a redefinition of marriage? In every culture, for thousands of years marriage has been defined as a lifetime commitment between a man and a woman. The only exception has been polygamy.

Never, though, has marriage been defined as a same-sex union. Now, in the twenty-first century, some so-called enlightened men and women have decided that society and laws should be changed to redefine marriage.

The idea of marriage originated with God when He created man and woman. In its origin, marriage was intended to be between one man and one woman. God's Word gives two reasons for the ideal: companionship and procreation. You can read more about it in Genesis 1–2, the first book of the Bible. Thus began the family as God intended.

Has twenty-first century man become so arrogant and selfish that we can redefine what God has ordained? I hope not.

Homosexuality, Marriage and the Church

"The precepts of the LORD are right . . ."
—Psalm 19:8

The idea of redefining marriage within the church to include same-sex unions is really an issue about biblical authority and interpretation:

- Is Scripture God's word, or man's word about God?
- Is Scripture true, or is it filled with errors?
- Does Scripture reveal absolute truth, or simply general principles?

Jesus said this about Scripture: "Do not think that I came to abolish the law of the prophets. I did not come to abolish but to fulfill." He later stated in a prayer to His heavenly Father, "Thy word is truth."

If Jesus is wrong about Scripture, He's surely not worthy to be called the Son of God. We may as well do what we want.

But if He is the perfect Son of God, then He is right about Scripture. This means Scripture is trustworthy and true. Our calling is to believe and obey God's Word as truth. It's not easy and we all fall short, but believing God's Word is always best.

DANG, I DID IT AGAIN

*". . . for I am not practicing what I would like to do
but I am doing the very thing I hate."*
—Romans 7:15

Dang, I did it again! The very thing I thought I had licked in my life, I did it again. Is that how you feel about a sin or a bad habit you just can't seem to overcome?

You are not alone. All of us are born with a sinful nature, a sinful bent. Sure, we are a creation of God that He said is very good. But we've all been poisoned by sin and are incapable of overcoming this poison in our own strength. The fact is, we need a cure, a doctor; we need to be saved from this deadly condition.

The good news is we can be. That's why God became a man in the person of Jesus. He is the Great Physician and came to save us from this deadly poison of sin. He forgives us and gives us the power to overcome what we can't defeat in our own strength.

He provides the Holy Spirit to do what we ought to do by giving us the inner desire and discipline to want to. It's found through faith—faith in Jesus Christ. He gives us the victory that we can never give ourselves.

January 29

AMERICA'S FAVORITE MEMORY VERSE

"The mind of a man plans his way,
but the LORD directs his steps."
—Proverbs 16:9

Do you know what seems to be America's favorite memory verse? "God helps those who help themselves." People say it all the time, usually in the form of friendly advice. What people don't realize is that this verse is not in the Bible. It was given to us by good ole Ben Franklin.

But it sounds so good and makes so much sense, common sense, that many people believe it as truth. In the process we can get in God's way: trying to help God out by doing things we feel need to be done. We may get results by taking matters into our own hands, but it surely isn't faith. Real faith means trusting God and doing things His way.

Yes, I know. God gave us a brain to use to make wise decisions. But taking matters into our own hands is not faith. If you've made a mess of things by buying into Ben Franklin's philosophy more than God's Word, seek the Lord's forgiveness and ask for God's help in cleaning up the mess.

I'm Just Curious

*". . . being darkened in their understanding, excluded from the
life of God because of the ignorance that is in them,
because of the hardness of their heart . . ."*
—Ephesians 4:18

I'm just curious . . .

Why is it, in a culture increasingly obsessed with the environment and protecting all species, that so many of these same folks are for destroying the lives of unborn children?

I'm just curious . . .

Why is it that values-free sex education, which is about teaching safe sex to save lives, is advising young people on an unsafe approach that could kill them? Entrusting your life to a thin rubber shield, when the failure rate is so high, is bewildering indeed.

I'm just curious . . .

Why is it, in a culture where the supreme virtue is often tolerance, that so many are so intolerant of the name of Jesus Christ or biblical convictions?

Don't things like this make you just a little bit curious too?

January 31

BABY BOOMERS

"You open Your hand and satisfy the desires of every living thing."
—Psalm 145:16

There were over seventy million of us born between 1946 and 1964. We are called Baby Boomers. No group in American history has ever been so studied and analyzed. And, because we consume over fifty-one percent of all products, no company can overlook us. What a humble bunch we are!

Leith Anderson writes, "Boomers operate differently and expect to be treated differently. Those who are Baby Boomers instinctively understand this."

What are some of the character traits of boomers?

- Quality. They shop for it. They'll drive to it.
- Choices. They prefer shopping malls, superstores, and 500 channels on the TV.
- Time. They will spend money on DSL, cell phones, and email, whatever it takes to save time.
- Low on commitment and loyalty. Their attitudes about marriages, jobs, and churches reflect this.
- Selfishness. They tend to be on a constant quest for self-fulfillment.

Boomers, as you hit mid-life with a vengeance, remember—God knows you best. Look to Him to find the ultimate quality relationship, to learn how to make the most of your time, to learn commitment, to discover Godly values, and to find the key to lasting fulfillment.

February 1

THE FIRST TEMPTATION

And [the serpent] said to the woman, "Indeed, has God said,
'You shall not eat from any tree of the garden'?"
—**Genesis 3:1**

Let's talk about temptation. Go back to the big one, the first one—the Devil tempting Eve in the Garden of Eden. Have you ever read the passage in Genesis 3? Note what he does:

1. He raises questions about the trustworthiness of God's Word.
2. The seeds of doubt are planted in Eve's mind.
3. When Eve says she's not to eat of the fruit or she'll die, the Devil replies cunningly, "You surely shall not die."

The ultimate liar accuses God of lying. He makes his word seem true and God's word seem unbelievable.

Think about temptation in your own life. It usually means believing your way is better than God's way. For Eve and for all of us, when we begin to doubt the Bible is reliable for living life the best way, we begin to give in to temptation—we buy into the lies and half-truths of the world.

For Eve and for all of us, it leads to spiritual death. Decide to believe God's Word—it is the best way. Ask God to give you strength to live it and resist temptation.

Plane Crash

"For to me, to live is Christ, and to die is gain."
—Philippians 1:21

We were dropping out of the sky—five people in a twin-engine Cessna. The right engine had gone out, and then the left followed. We knew that within a minute or two we would crash. I thought of my wife and our three-month-old son. Would he grow up without a father?

I prayed that God would guide the pilot in bringing us down. Amazingly, in a way I can't explain, a peace came over me, a sureness that we would be OK whether we lived or died, because we knew Christ.

We crashed in a rice field. Part of the left wing broke off and we belly-flopped and spun to a stop; yet we all walked away unharmed, a miracle for sure. But the greater miracle was to be face-to-face with death and unafraid. That meant everything.

If you were in my seat, how would you have felt? The good news is with Jesus Christ, we can face death knowing that if we live or die—we live.

TRUSTING GOD

"And those who know Your name will put their trust in You,
for You, O LORD, have not forsaken those who seek You."
—Psalm 9:10

Isn't it amazing all the people we entrust our lives to every week? We trust pharmacists to give us the right pills from a prescription we can't read. We trust pilots we don't know to fly us to the right destination, believing they know how to fly that baby exactly where we need to go. As we sit in traffic on the interstate, we trust our lives to engineers and road construction crews, believing the bridges will hold.

Yet people have trouble trusting God.

They often say, "I can't see Him." Do we see the engineers who designed the bridge? Do we know the pilots? Not usually. Yet God, our Creator who loves us more than anyone, who even sacrificed His Son for us to have forgiveness of sin and eternal life, is difficult to trust.

It's amazing. It doesn't make sense to trust imperfect men and not to trust a perfect God.

February 4

SPIRITUAL WIMPS

"He must be one who manages his own household well, keeping his children under control with all dignity . . ."
—1 Timothy 3:4

When are men the biggest wimps?

It often amazes me that men who are good athletes, or who pride themselves on hard work and self-reliance, are absolute wimps when it comes to fulfilling God's calling of being the spiritual leader in the home. Many macho men are classic spiritual wimps in this area. They look at religion and church as mostly women's stuff and often rely on the wife and mother to fill the void of spiritual leadership in the family. The guys simply wimp out.

But Scripture is clear. The father is to have this major responsibility. There is no doubt that a primary reason for the disintegration of the family is that so many men are spiritual wimps rather than spiritual leaders.

If you're a husband or a father, stop wimping out on what it means to be a man in God's eyes. Ask the Lord for guidance for what it means to be a spiritual leader. Come on men, rise to the challenge! The future of our land is depending on you.

CHURCH-GOING PHONIES

"Behold, I am insignificant; what can I reply to You?
I lay my hand on my mouth . . ."
—Job 40:4

I want to write to you church-going phonies—the ones who look heavenly on Sunday, but live like hell Monday through Saturday. You look good on the outside but when God looks at your inside, your heart, it's a dirty mess!

I've got bad news for you. Jesus hates religious phoniness. But there's good news. He loves the phonies. He gave His life for phony hypocrites like you and me.

The end of being a church-going phony is to admit our sin separates us from God; then ask Christ's forgiveness and believe He is our only hope for change, to be right with God.

And here's the irony: when we begin to be more real with God and others, we begin to be more like Jesus. He's the only person who ever lived without any trace of phoniness.

February 6

THE RIGHT VALUES

"... I WILL PUT MY LAWS UPON THEIR HEART, AND
ON THEIR MIND I WILL WRITE THEM."
—Hebrews 10:16

There's a lot of talk about values, like family values or traditional values. The cover of Newsweek magazine recently asked, "Whose Values?"

Let me offer a suggestion; it's very old but very contemporary. How about the values from man's Creator—from God Himself?

They go like this:

- You shall have no other gods before Me.
- You shall not make for yourself an idol.
- You shall not take the name of the Lord your God in vain.
- Remember the Sabbath day.
- Honor your father and mother.
- You shall not murder.
- You shall not commit adultery.
- You shall not steal.
- You shall not bear false witness.
- You shall not covet.

These are not suggestions for when you feel they are appropriate. They are absolute commands. They tell us how to live life to the fullest.

Whose values?

I encourage you to adopt God's Big Ten. You'll find they are key to living life to the fullest.

A Summary of the Big Ten

*"YOU SHALL LOVE THE LORD YOUR GOD WITH ALL
YOUR HEART, AND WITH ALL YOUR SOUL,
AND WITH ALL YOUR MIND."*
—**Matthew 22:37–39**

I believe the Ten Commandments are a great guide for successful living. The Big Ten are the ultimate foundation on which to base spiritual and ethical behavior. The first four commandments focus on our relationship with God. The last six deal with our relationship to our fellow man. In short, right spirituality leads to right living with our fellow man.

The first four are: 1) put God first, 2) have no idols, 3) respect His name, and 4) have a weekly Sabbath. The last six are: 5) don't murder, 6) don't commit adultery, 7) don't steal, 8) don't bear false witness, 9) don't lie, and 10) don't covet your neighbor's possessions.

These are stated so negatively, like a bunch of don'ts. And when someone says, "Don't," something within us makes us want to do it. Jesus summarized them positively. I like His best.

He said, "Love God with all your heart, soul, and mind" (the first four in a nutshell). And He said, "Love your neighbor as yourself" (the last six, in five words). Wow! The perfect summary of the Big Ten.

Both versions, the Big Ten or the Big Two, teach us how to be in right relationship with God and right relationships with our fellow man. When we get right with God, we'll be right with our fellow man.

February 8

A LIVE APPEARANCE AFTER DEATH

"Reach here with your finger, and see My hands; and reach here
your hand and put it into My side; and do not be unbelieving,
but believing."
—**John 20:27**

In the movie *The Sixth Sense*, Bruce Willis plays a psychiatrist who works with a young boy who sees dead people. The movie stirs the viewer to feel the horrifying fear of the young boy. Seeing a dead person would frighten anyone. In that light, it's little wonder the disciples of Jesus were initially terrified when He appeared to them after His death. They had no illusions about His death. They had been hiding in fear of the authorities who might kill them if they were found to be followers of Jesus.

The authorities ordered them to stop preaching the heretical nonsense, but they could not stop telling what they knew to be true. All but one died a martyr's death for proclaiming these facts. Death caused them no fear.

After their initial fear, they found peace. They knew He was God, and they devoted their lives to sharing this Good News and their faith in Him. So can we.

No event in history is more important than Jesus' resurrection. Do you believe it?

February 9

MAKING THE CUT

". . . if anyone's name was not found written in the book of life,
he was thrown into the lake of fire."
—Revelation 20:15

I remember it like it was yesterday. I was walking to the coach's office to read who made the cut for the basketball team. If your name wasn't on the door, you hadn't made the cut.

I was stunned! Where was my name? I had played basketball all my life. I was devastated to find my name was left off the list.

God's Word in Revelation 20 tells us that when Jesus returns, all mankind will be divided into two lists: Those who make the cut will spend eternity on God's team and have their names written in the Book of Life. All who don't will spend eternity separated from God. Their names will be listed in the book of deeds and they'll be devastated.

What's the difference?

The Book of Life contains the names of people with repentant faith in Jesus Christ as their Savior and Lord. Those in the book of deeds will be people trying to make the cut by being good. None of us are good enough for heaven. We have to be perfect. But there is One who is perfect. His name is Jesus and He is our only hope of making the cut.

Which book are you in?

Slight Edge

"Finally then, brethren, we request and exhort you in the Lord Jesus, that as you receive from us instruction as to how you ought to walk and please God . . . that you excel still more."
—1 Thessalonians 4:1

Every time the Olympics comes around, I'm always amazed at the small difference in time between the winner of the gold and the other competitors. It's called the slight edge. In some races it will be a difference of just hundredths of a second. Yet, we remember the winners and tend to forget the also-rans.

In the game of life, so often the difference between being an also-ran and the winner is that slight edge. The difference between being average and great is just a little bit of difference, just a little extra effort.

Because life is a challenge for us all, I urge you to think about a personal relationship with God to find that slight edge for living. Faith in God provides strength and character to give us just the little bit of extra required to have a successful life. What a difference in the end between being average and being great.

February 11

FINDING THE RIGHT MATE

"He who finds a wife finds a good thing . . ."
—Proverbs 18:22

Everybody wants to make the right choice in choosing a mate. What a nightmare if we don't. What a blessing if we do. If you are in a serious relationship, ask yourself these questions:

- Is this person my best friend? If not, you're not ready.
- Do we share common faith and values? If not, you'll have conflict and drift apart.
- Do family and friends affirm the relationship? Choosing a mate means choosing a family.
- Am I willing to make a lifetime commitment? Marriage is not for trying out. That's a sure road to divorce.
- Do I want this person to be the parent of my children?
- Do I wake up to every day wanting to be with them versus convincing myself why I like them?

If you can say yes to each of these, you may have found the right one. If not, you may want to slow down or even call it off. But most of all, seek God's will through prayer and be willing to follow His lead in one of life's biggest decisions.

What Love Is

*"We know love by this, that He laid down His life for us;
and we ought to lay down our lives for the brethren."*
—1 John 3:16

Dr. Michael DeBakey, the famous heart surgeon, once received a letter from an eleven-year-old girl with this question, "Is there any love in an artificial heart?" Love is elusive, yet we long for it.

How would you define love? Most everyone knows it is real, but who can really describe it?

I can't define love, but God's Word sure can. The Bible reminds us that love is patient and kind, not envious, selfish, or arrogant. Love doesn't keep records when people let us down or do us wrong. Love forgives. Love is happy for others' successes. Love is very optimistic. Love bears all things; it believes in others and what they can be, thus putting up with a lot. Love hopes for the best in others. True love never gives up; it just keeps on keeping on; it means a commitment to love a person whether they love us or not.

Is love found in an artificial heart? I'm afraid not, but love can be found in an old heart made new by the power of the Great Physician, Jesus Christ.

HUSBANDS, LOVE YOUR WIVES

"Husbands, love your wives . . ."
—Colossians 3:19

Husbands, what our wives need most from us is love. But there are several aspects of love that most men don't come by naturally. One is the woman's need for romance, attention, and affection. I know what some of you guys are thinking: "Hey, I like sex; I'll meet that need." If that is your thinking, you're clueless!

Husbands, remember that with our wives, romance and affection is much more than sex. It's how we treat her throughout the day. It's saying words like, "I love you" and "I need you." It's a listening ear. It's remembering special days like anniversaries, birthdays, and Valentine's Day. It's weekly dates and overnight getaways—times of falling in love all over again.

God's Word says, "Husbands, love your wives." Just remember that love means romance, affection, attention, and not just sex.

CASUAL LOVE

"But God demonstrates His own love toward us,
in that while we were yet sinners, Christ died for us."
—Romans 5:8

Love.
How often we use the word. We love warm weather. We love our husband or wife. We love our college football team. We love the latest fashion trend. We speak the word in our most tender moments and then use it to describe our feelings about a flavor of ice cream.

Do you know that you are loved? Really loved?

The God who created all of life loves you even if you don't love Him in return. He doesn't wait for you to demonstrate your love for Him. He loves you first. He clearly demonstrated His love through Jesus Christ, especially when Christ gave His life for us.

Over the next few days, try to notice how many times the word love is used in casual conversation. Each time you hear it, think about the love of God—real love. Think of how much He loves you and begin to experience His love. When you begin to know His love, you'll be amazed at the joy in your life.

Can't Legislate Morality

*"But we know that the Law is good, if one uses it lawfully,
realizing the fact that law is not made for a righteous person,
but for those who are lawless and rebellious . . ."*
—1 Timothy 1:8–9

One of the leaders of the Georgia General Assembly, in opposition to House ethics legislation, was quoted as saying, "You can't legislate morality."

Have you ever used the argument that you can't legislate morality?

I ask: why do those guys meet? To make laws! Has there ever been a law written that wasn't legislating morality? They all do. Yeah, I know what they mean: laws don't guarantee proper behavior. Any law can be broken, but laws sure do make people think twice before breaking them.

Laws of the state are part of God's plan to protect man from himself and from others. So the next time someone says you can't legislate morality, just suggest they do away with laws on rape, murder, and robbery.

Sure, laws don't change a person's heart, only Jesus Christ can do that, but they do help to protect us from our fellow man, and our fellow man from us.

TURNING EVIL INTO GOOD

"As for you, you meant evil against me, but God meant it for good in order to bring about this present result . . ."
—**Genesis 50:20**

One of the great stories of the Bible deals with the life of Joseph, the son of Jacob. He was loved by his father and resented by his ten older brothers. They sold him into slavery and told their father he had been killed and devoured by a wild animal.

What is so amazing about Joseph is that he never gave up and never quit trusting in God, even though he faced setback after setback. He was falsely accused and unjustly thrown into prison. Miraculously, one day Joseph was called to interpret Pharaoh's dreams. In so doing, he was appointed prime minister of Egypt to save the people from famine.

Amazingly, because he saved the people from famine, the brothers who betrayed him were saved as well. When they realized the prime minister of Egypt was the brother they had betrayed years earlier, they were afraid. Yet Joseph forgave them and said, "What you meant for evil, God meant for good."

What faith—what forgiveness—what an example for all of us.

February 17

SEXUAL REVOLUTION

"But put on the Lord Jesus Christ,
and make no provision for the flesh in regard to its lusts."
—Romans 13:14

The 1960's ushered in the sexual revolution. They called it the new morality, but it wasn't new; it was very old. The Greeks and Romans embraced it thousands of years ago, and soon afterwards they were history. It was introduced thousands of years before that in the days of Noah. At that time, God got so disgusted with the filth that He gave the earth a good bath.

How is the sexual revolution progressing in the twenty-first century?

The latter part of the twentieth century ushered in an epidemic of sexually transmitted diseases—some of them like AIDS are deadly. The sexual fears began to multiply. To save the revolution, the idea of safe sex was introduced, but it wasn't safe—it was just as deadly. So much for utopian dreams!

When you think about it, the sexual revolution has been a disaster. Countless lives have been lost and countless others are disillusioned with the emptiness. That's why God gave a warning when He invented sex. It's great, but only as an expression of love between a man and woman in marriage. That's revolutionary! The ultimate safe sex.

CREATION

"In the beginning God created the heavens and the earth."
—Genesis 1:1

How do you think life came about? Where did it all begin? How was it all put in motion?

Some believe life evolved by chance; others believe all creation came from God. The fact is, both philosophies take a great deal of faith.

Imagine this: One of our soldiers in the Middle East sets off a landmine and out of the explosion comes a perfectly built 747, ready to fly him home to America. Would you believe that story? It would take a great deal of faith. And yet, it takes that much faith and more to believe that all life evolved by chance because all life is far more complex than a 747.

Look around you—the birth of a baby, the predictable seasons, the beauty of spring. Do you have enough faith to believe it happened by chance?

I don't. I'm going to put my bet on God. He put it all in motion.

PATIENCE WITH OTHERS

"Patience of spirit is better than haughtiness of spirit."
—Ecclesiastes 7:8

To have patience with other people is one of life's greatest qualities.

In *Lincoln, the War Years,* Sandberg writes of Lincoln's patience with his cabinet in the most difficult days of American history. Many in his cabinet felt they were a whole lot smarter than the president. They made a point of letting other people know it, too. Some mocked and belittled him; one even called him a dumb gorilla. These words often got back to President Lincoln and his wife. She despised them; yet, he was incredibly patient. When he died, these same men realized they had served under one of the greatest Americans who had ever lived.

Patience with others is a Christ-like quality. Ask God for patience but watch out if you do! God just might put some difficult people around you to try your patience. This is a part of learning patience and an answer to your prayer.

Destroying Our Enemies

"You have heard that it was said, 'YOU SHALL LOVE YOUR NEIGHBOR and hate your enemy.' But I say to you, 'Love your enemies and pray for those who persecute you . . .'"
—Matthew 5:43–44

The word enemy has been defined as anyone who is not for us. In light of that definition, we can all think of folks we work with, cross paths with, and sometimes even live with, who are not for us. Yet, Jesus Christ said, "Love your enemies." To love our friends is not unique, but to love our enemies is.

At the end of the Civil War, many Northerners were demanding that the South be punished for the devastation the war had caused the United States. Feeling he was too soft on the South, a group visited President Lincoln at the White House. One man became so intense that he pounded on Mr. Lincoln's desk and said, "Mr. President, I believe in destroying my enemies."

President Lincoln reflected a moment, then slowly stood and said, "Do we not destroy our enemies when we make them our friends?"

That is the spirit of Christianity that literally changes the world. The key question is—is it you?

February 21

WISDOM IN INVESTING AND SAVING

"Do not store up for yourselves treasures on earth . . .
but store up for yourselves treasures in heaven."
—Matthew 6:19–20

Savings and investments seem to be on everybody's mind. There are news channels that, all day long, focus solely on the market. There are newspapers, magazines, and newsletters that deal exclusively with money and investments.

What is the right starting point on investing? God's Word tells us our starting point should be eternity. If all our focus is on earthly investing, we are mighty shortsighted. Eternity is a lot longer than anything in this life.

Jesus tells us that when we invest in eternal treasure, we never lose it. It has returns that last forever. We should begin with investments in eternity even before we focus on investments for college, retirement, or in whatever else we're investing. This takes faith, but it proves to God where our hearts are—whether with Him or with our money.

Many men who see themselves as strong are absolutely gutless in this area. It takes a strong man to have this kind of faith. Wisdom in investing truly begins with the long-term view of eternity.

REASON FOR LIVING

". . . He who began a good work in you will perfect it
until the day of Christ Jesus."
—Philippians 1:6

Most everyone is interested in discovering their purpose for living—the reason for being born, the reason for existing.

I have good news. God has put that desire within you, for as your Creator, He has a purpose and plan for your life. Your role is to discover it and use the gifts, talents, and opportunities God has given you to make the most of your life. God's ultimate purpose is that everyone would have a personal relationship with Him through faith in Jesus Christ. And everyone can—through faith.

Then there is more good news. God's Word says, "I am confident . . . that He who began a good work in you will carry it to completion until the day of Jesus' coming."

What a promise! Once we put our life and trust in God, He promises He'll begin to reveal our life purpose to us. He will also provide the power needed to see that we get it done. What are you waiting for? It's time to discover your reason for living and live it out.

THE MEANING OF MAN

"Then God said, 'Let Us make man in Our image,
according to Our likeness . . .'"
—Genesis 1:26

What is the meaning of man?

The answer is on page one of the Bible. It says "and God created man in His own image." What does it mean to be in the image of God? It doesn't mean physical appearance, but it does mean in God's likeness.

We can think like God. We can reason. We are creative.

We are to rule over creation. We need to care for it, protect it, and use it in a way that is pleasing to God.

We are spiritual beings. Unlike the animals, we can worship God. God desires a personal relationship with us.

We are moral beings. Man deals with right and wrong. The best way for us to do this is to obey God's Word in faith.

If we submit to God, we reflect His nature. But when we don't, we look more like beasts. Understanding this, does your life reflect the image of God or are you more like an animal?

Meaning of Man, Part 2

"Then the Lord God formed man of dust from the ground,
and breathed into his nostrils the breath of life;
and man became a living being."
—Genesis 2:7

The first two chapters of the Bible explain the meaning of man.

- Man is distinct from the animals. We're made in the image of God. We can think abstractly like God. We can reason, create, and appreciate beauty and moral order.
- We're to be fruitful and multiply in the context of marriage. Sex is a great gift invented by God for mutual enjoyment and procreation, but for marriage only.
- We're called to rule over creation. We are to care for the environment and all of God's creation. We are His managers, with a great responsibility.
- We're to maintain balance between work and rest. Work is a gift—a key to fulfillment—to be done for God's glory. But God initiated a day of rest as well.
- We are created to have a relationship with God through trust and obedience. When we don't, we mess it up big time.

HYPOCRITES

"Therefore be imitators of God, as beloved children . . ."
—Ephesians 5:1

Of the major objections to Christianity, this one is still at the top of the charts: "I'm not interested in Christianity or the church because the church is a bunch of hypocrites and I don't want anything to do with them."

It might surprise people who've made a statement like that to know that they are right. The church *is* full of hypocrites, but I can't think of a better place for a bunch of hypocrites to be than in church. You see, the church is not a hotel for saints; it's a hospital for sinners. It's a place where people go when they recognize they need help.

Let me encourage you to do this: instead of blaming Jesus Christ for the shortcomings of His followers, I challenge you to look at the person of Christ in Scripture. You'll find no hypocrisy in Him. Look at the person of Christ and you'll find the most genuine person who has ever lived.

JOY

"A joyful heart is good medicine,
but a broken spirit dries up the bones."
—**Proverbs 17:22**

Do you need a good dose of joy? It really is good medicine. Years ago, *Psychology Today* magazine published an article, "Laugh and Be Well." In the article, Norman Cousin wrote about a remarkable recovery from a disabling condition through massive doses of vitamin C and comedy clips. His experience spawned a new field of scientific research studying how the brain influences the immune system.

Funny, the Bible has said the same thing all along. In Proverbs, God's Word says, "A cheerful heart is good medicine, but a crushed spirit dries up the bones." Do you need a good dose of joy, yet nothing seems to ease the pain?

I have good news. You can find joy. It is found in a person who is the source of a lasting joy that overcomes the heartaches of life. His name is Jesus.

Jesus says, "I've told you these things, that My joy may be in you, and that your joy may be made full."

We all need to enjoy laughter. It's good medicine. But lasting joy is only found in Jesus.

February 27

Follow Me

"... If anyone wishes to come after Me, he must deny himself,
and take up his cross daily and follow Me."
—Luke 9:23

When Jesus called His disciples, His first command before He told them their mission was, "Follow Me."

What does it mean to follow someone?

Imagine that you are in an unfamiliar place following a friend in your car. To get where you are going, you have to:

- Trust them to get you where you need to go.
- Submit to their leadership; otherwise you get lost.
- Keep your eyes on them; if you lose sight of them, you'll get lost.
- Go at their pace, not get ahead or fall behind.

This is what is involved in following Jesus, too.

We have to trust Him to guide us where we need to go. We have to submit to His leadership, His will before our own. We have to stay focused on Him and go at His pace. If we do this, He'll lead us where we need to go. And here's even more good news—in the process He'll reveal to us our life purpose.

February 28

RISING TO CONQUER

"I can do all things through Him who strengthens me."
—Philippians 4:13

Do you ever wonder why certain people rise to meet a great challenge and others don't? Have you heard the story of David and Goliath?

If ever there was a giant challenge, David found it in Goliath, a hardened warrior who was nine-and-a-half-feet tall and filled his enemies with terror. Yet David, just a teenage shepherd, was willing to take him on. His people thought he was crazy but he had faith in the Lord and remembered how God had strengthened him in the past.

He said, "When a lion or bear came and took a lamb from my flock, I went after it and struck the beast and killed it. The Lord who delivered me from the power of the lion and the bear will deliver me from this giant."

And He did. David slew Goliath. He faced a giant challenge and was victorious because he had been faithful day by day.

When the big public challenges come, we'll be ready if we're faithful to God in the various behind-the-scenes daily tasks. It's the faithfulness in the small things that is key to meeting life's giant challenges victoriously.

March 1

MATT

"... It is not those who are healthy who need a physician,
but those who are sick."
—Matthew 9:12

One of the things I love most about Jesus is His love for all people, even those people many religious folks don't want to be around. One of those people was His disciple Matthew. He later became one of Jesus' biographers.

Matt was one of the last guys you'd want on your team if you were trying to impress good religious folks. He was a crook. He ran with a bad crowd. He was a party animal. But after Jesus reached out to him and asked him to join His team, Matt was so excited he threw a party for all his wild and notorious friends, just to meet Jesus. And they all had a great time.

But the religious crowd was appalled. They thought, "If Jesus is supposed to be a man of God, why would He run with such a rough crowd?"

Jesus responded, "It's not the healthy who need a doctor. I came for those who know they're sinners and need help—not for those who think they're righteous."

Don't you love it? You may be one of those folks like Matt, and I hope you'll remember that Jesus loves you.

March 2

HUSBANDS SHOW LOVE THROUGH UNDERSTANDING

"Make your ear attentive to wisdom,
incline your heart to understanding."
—Proverbs 2:2

God's Word commands husbands to love their wives, and one way the Bible tells us to show that love is through understanding. Most guys are blockheads in this area. Understanding our wives is not our strong suit.

For many years, my wife would share a problem with me. I thought that she was looking for advice or a solution, and like an idiot, I gave it to her. She would express frustration with me and I'd respond by saying, "Well, why did you ask me for help?"

She would look at me like "you blockhead", which is exactly what I was. It took years to realize she didn't want advice or a solution: she wanted understanding, a listening ear, empathy. I'm getting better.

Husbands, are you showing understanding to your wife? It may not be your strong suit, but it sure does show her that you love her.

March 3

A Man in Full

"... be made complete, be comforted, be like-minded,
live in peace ..."
—2 Corinthians 13:11

For much of early 1999, Tom Wolfe's *A Man in Full* was a bestseller. Though superficial, it's a great read. Like so many real people in Atlanta, the fictional characters' lives are based on money, power, and sex. Yet Wolfe's genius helps us to see ourselves.

It's a story of a fictional real estate tycoon who created quite a stir in Atlanta. People wondered, who is the man in full, the man who pursues money, power, and sex with gusto? Yet, as time marches on, he struggles to hang on. After a life of prideful self-reliance, Wolfe's man in full winds up pitifully dependent.

I have a question. What is "a man in full?" A real man? A man's man?

I propose to you that the real "man in full" is the complete man— emotionally, physically, intellectually, and spiritually. He is a whole man. He becomes a real man in God's eyes when he seeks to be God's man.

The only perfect man in full faced death head-on and He whipped it. He started with a small group and now He's the leader of billions. No one can move men to live right like He can. His power is unsurpassed. His initials are "J. C." He is some kind of man!

He's the only perfect "man in full" for He is the supernatural man. He's the only one who can take an ordinary man and transform him into a real man—a true "man in full."

March 4

INFLATION THAT CALLS FOR DEFLATION

". . . I say to everyone among you not to think more highly
of himself than he ought to think . . ."
—Romans 12:3

There's a story of a British general serving in Asia who hosted a dinner party for distinguished guests. One of those guests was an aristocratic lady visiting from England. The general's assistant seated her to his left while the highest seat of honor was to his right. She seethed inside and as the dinner wore on, she could not contain herself. She haughtily complained to the general, "I guess you have difficulty finding qualified help to seat people properly."

To which the general replied, "Not at all. Those who matter don't mind and those who mind, don't matter."

Her ego was suffering from inflation that called for deflation. It's a reminder of the danger of prideful arrogance. The more our ego gets inflated, the more life has a way of humbling us—big time. God's Word tells us to not think more highly of ourselves than we ought, for ego inflation leads to ego deflation in the most humiliating ways.

March 5

WHEN THE CLOUDS COME IN

"Jesus Christ is the same yesterday and today and forever."
—Hebrews 13:8

Years ago, my wife and I visited the base of the Matterhorn in Switzerland on a beautiful day. It has to be one of the most majestic sights on earth. When we woke up the next morning, I walked out of our room to view the Matterhorn once again and it was gone. Absolutely no evidence it was there. The clouds had rolled in. When the clouds lifted, it was obvious the mountain had not moved.

Sometimes it's like that with God. We come to experience Him in an awe-inspiring way. But later the clouds of life roll in: disappointment, rejection, suffering. It's like God is nowhere near.

But remember, He has not moved. He's as sure and as near as the Matterhorn was to us that day in Switzerland when we could not see it. So when the clouds move in, it's time to show God you really do have faith. For in time, the clouds of life will lift and you'll see that God has not moved—He was there all along.

OBEDIENCE

**"If you keep My commandments, you will abide in My love;
just as I have kept My Father's commandments
and abide in His love."
—John 15:10**

Parents, what is the greatest proof of your children's love for you? Is it when they say they love you? That's great, but it's not proof. Really, it's when they obey you—willingly.

Many people miss this truth. They say they love God, maybe even go to church regularly, but there is little evidence of real love for God in their lives.

A recent poll showed that eighty percent of Americans believe that the Bible is the inspired Word of God. That same poll reflected that more than seventy percent felt every individual has to decide right or wrong for himself. That's saying one thing and doing another.

Jesus said, "If you love Me, you will keep My commandments." The proof of our love is our willingness to obey God and His commands. Doesn't it make you feel great when your child willingly obeys you? Why don't you give God the same joy? Obey Him because it's your desire to do so. Love Him like you want to be loved by your own child.

March 7

CLONING

*"God created man in His own image,
in the image of God He created him . . ."*
—Genesis 1:27

Cloning is one of the eerie developments of modern technology. Taking the DNA of one person and replicating it in the life of another could lead to tremendous medical advances and horrendous possibilities.

In 1932, Aldous Huxley published his book, *Brave New World*. Although his grandfather and brother were world-renowned scientists, Huxley took a different approach. In his book, he foresaw a society with a one-world government where science and government worked together to determine the destiny of man-made men. 1932? What insight! We're getting there fast.

With cloning on the horizon for humans, Huxley's concerns have become a distinct possibility. Yet, when man plays God, he always winds up acting more like a beast than someone created in God's image.

Science can enhance man's quality of life, and science can help us understand God's creation. But science is not to play God—science must answer to God. God's desire is for every life to be distinct with His unique purpose and plan. This is one area I'd rather leave in the hands of God than in the hands of science.

March 8

POWER

"Blessed are the gentle, for they shall inherit the earth."
—Matthew 5:5

Do you have it? Do you want it? What are you willing to do to get it?

The misuse of power is a constant reality. People have a tendency to sacrifice anything or anyone to attain and retain influence. How many relationships have been damaged because one person took advantage of his or her position of power? How much disappointment and heartache could be avoided if people with power had the correct perspective on how it should be exercised?

The most powerful person who ever lived is Jesus Christ. He gives us the picture of the proper use of power. Although He could have commanded whatever He wanted, He chose to live a life of sacrifice and servanthood, as exemplified on the cross. In the process, He accomplished what He set out to do—to become the Savior of the world.

Because of His life, death, and resurrection, you and I can use His power for good. Now that's real power!

March 9

THEORIES ON THE RESURRECTION

". . . I am the first and the last, and the living One . . .
I am alive forevermore . . ."
—Revelation 1:17–18

Do you want to disprove Christianity?
The key to doing this is to prove that Jesus Christ did not rise from the dead. You prove that and Christianity is a joke.

In the 1930's, a British lawyer by the name of Frank Morrison took on that challenge. He was convinced the resurrection was a myth. Using his skills as a lawyer, he sought to do the world a favor by exposing this fraud once and for all.

He began to study the evidence, examining it just as he would in court. In the course of his work, an amazing thing occurred. This skeptic began to realize the evidence for the resurrection of Jesus was so strong it had to be true. As a result, the first chapter of his book, *Who Moved the Stone?*, was titled "The Book That Refused to Be Written."

How about you? Have you examined the evidence objectively? I urge you to consider the evidence, then decide—fact or fiction?

HOPE AFTER DIVORCE

". . . we have fixed our hope on the living God,
who is the Savior of all men, especially of believers."
—1 Timothy 4:10

Very often people who face divorce feel hopeless. Sadly, many who turn to the church for help feel rejected, not welcomed. Many have told me they felt outcast and shunned, even if they were the spouse left behind. Sometimes this is a perception, but sometimes it is very real. Tragically, the Christian army is the only army in the world known to shoot its wounded.

Yes, Scripture teaches that God hates divorce, but just because He hates divorce doesn't mean He hates the divorcee. He loves the divorcee. God hates divorce for many of the same reasons the divorcee hates divorce—most of all, for the pain and suffering it causes in so many lives. There is no doubt that divorce always results from sin, but it is not the unforgivable sin.

Divorce is never what God wants, but Jesus teaches us that we have a God of second chances—a God of forgiveness. When we trust in Christ and confess our sins to the Lord, we begin to realize He loves us and forgives us completely. We can find that total and complete healing in the person of Jesus Christ.

March 11

WORLD VIEWS SECULARISM, ISLAM, AND CHRISTIANITY— THREE COMPETING VIEWS

*"Now if Christ is preached,
that He has been raised from the dead,
how do some among you say that
there is no resurrection of the dead?"*
—1 Corinthians 15:12

Secularism often lumps Islam and Christianity together as being one and the same, seeing both as equal threats to their cherished worldview. Yet Islam and Christianity are radically different.

Followers of Islam tend to lump Christianity and secularism into one lost group. When they see the decadence of American media and entertainment and know that most Americans claim to be Christians, Muslims see a failed and corrupt religion.

Christianity sees Islam and secularism as radically different. But they share one common belief, the belief that Jesus is not God. They believe He was just a man and they don't believe He rose from the dead.

All of Christianity rises and falls on Jesus' resurrection. If He did, He's different from every man and every other worldview. If He didn't, Christianity is a colossal hoax based on a lie and you don't want to believe it.

So what do you believe? I've put my faith in Jesus.

LOYALTY AND DEVOTION

". . . where you go, I will go, and where you lodge,
I will lodge. Your people shall be my people,
and your God, my God."
—Ruth 1:16

Loyalty is a precious commodity. Many profess it, but few have it (especially when life goes sour). Yet there are few gifts greater than another person's loyalty, especially when we feel like the whole world is against us. Some relationships with in-laws are challenging because the only reason you have a loyalty to them is that you both love the same person. When that person is gone, there is often little to tie you together.

Ruth is one of the Bible's most inspiring women. Her mother-in-law, Naomi, lost her husband and her two sons. One of those sons was Ruth's husband. But listen to Ruth's words to Naomi: "Where you go, I will go. Where you lodge, I will lodge and your people shall be my people and your God, my God. And where you die, I will die and there I will be buried." She not only said it, she kept her word. Loyalty is a precious commodity, especially when life goes sour.

March 13

MARRIAGE AND CIVILIZATION

". . . This is now bone of my bones, and flesh of my flesh;
she shall be called Woman, because she was taken out of Man."
—Genesis 2:23

Even though every major religion has defined marriage as a lifetime commitment between a man and a woman, some in the twenty-first century want to redefine it. But even if you leave God out of the discussion, there are good reasons why mankind defined marriage that way:

1. *For the civilization of men.* Men have a tendency toward violence and to be animalistic when lustful passion strikes. Society has seen marriage as a protection against that.
2. *For the protection and security of women.* Men are physically stronger, and because of men's animalistic tendencies, marriage has historically been for the physical protection and security of women.
3. *For the welfare of the children.* Growing up in a family with a healthy and stable marriage between a man and a woman has been the best environment for a child's development and maturity. It's how children learn to deal with men and women responsibly and respectfully.

The civilization of men, the protection and security of women, and the welfare of children are three key reasons that marriage is to be between a man and a woman.

INNER PEACE

"For You have been a defense for the helpless . . .
a refuge from the storm . . ."
—Isaiah 25:4

A contest offered a valuable prize for the best illustration of the concept of peace. Many artists entered. There were renderings of beautiful sunsets over calm seas and hazy scenes of tranquil rivers in lush valleys. The prizewinner's depiction was very different from these tranquil scenes. Painted in black and gray, it depicted the terror of a violent storm. Lightning split the clouds; rain and hail pounded the ground. In the center of the painting was a storm-tossed oak tree. Holding on with all its might to one of the limbs of the tree was a little bird, singing at the top of its lungs. That's true peace.

Ultimate peace is not the *absence* of storms but inner peace *amidst* storms. And man never finds lasting inner peace until he finds peace with God. For when you find peace with God, you begin to experience peace within.

Have you found that peace? I hope you will. It begins with knowing Christ as Lord.

March 15

THE GOAL OF LIFE

"... I count all things to be loss in view of the surpassing value of knowing Christ Jesus my Lord ..."
—Philippians 3:8

What is the goal of life? What is *your* goal for life? What does God's Word say should be our goal for living?

Is it finding happiness? No.

Is it accomplishing much to leave a legacy? That can be good, but that's not it.

Is it being good and helping your fellow man? That's good, too, but there is something more.

Read the words of the apostle Paul: "I count all things to be loss in view of the surpassing value of knowing Christ Jesus my Lord, for whom I have suffered the loss of all things, and count them but rubbish in order that I may gain Christ."

Knowing Christ is the ultimate goal of life. If you know Christ, you don't have to worry about finding happiness, being good, helping your fellow man, or leaving a legacy. All of that flows out of knowing Christ. The ultimate goal of life is to know Christ. Do you really know Him?

March 16

How to Know Christ

"I will give them a heart to know Me, for I am the LORD . . ."
—Jeremiah 24:7

God's Word makes it clear—the goal of life is knowing Christ. Now think what knowing Christ *doesn't* mean. It doesn't mean knowing *about* Him.

I love to read biographies, especially of presidents. At the end of a great biography you feel like you know the person. Yet I've never met a president; I know a lot about them, but I've never known one personally. Most people know a lot *about* Jesus but that doesn't mean they know Him personally. So how can you know Him personally?

1. *God's Word.* Through His Word you can know Him. But Scripture without faith is just knowing *about* Him.
2. *Have faith.* That's key to believing what Scripture says is true.
3. *Pray.* Talking and listening to God allows you to know Him.
4. *Attend a Christ-centered church.* This helps you know Him through worship, fellowship, and ministry.

When it comes to Jesus, do you know Him or just know *about* Him? Really knowing Him makes all the difference.

ADVICE ABOUT RELIGION AND WHISKY

"For we also once were foolish ourselves . . . But when the kindness of God our Savior and His love for mankind appeared, He saved us . . ."
—Titus 3:3–4

Bryant," my daddy always told me, "religion and whisky are a lot alike—too much of either one will get the best of you." That was a co-worker's advice when he heard I had decided to leave the business world for the ministry.

I laughed and had to agree with him, for religion and whisky can get the best of you. Go overboard with either and you can mess up your life and others' too.

Jesus said to the Pharisees (who were very religious, guilt inducing, and self-righteous) that "their converts became twice the sons of hell that they were." Because Jesus knew religion can get the best of anyone, what He came to offer was a relationship, a healthy relationship, with God. Christianity is not about being religious but about having a relationship with God that gives meaning to your life.

If religion or whisky is getting the best of you, you might try Jesus and enjoy a healthy relationship with God.

March 18

REDEFINING GOD

"If you had known Me, you would have known My Father also . . ."
—John 14:7

A weekend edition of the *Wall Street Journal* ran an interesting article titled, "Redefining God," about how so many in our modern world are redefining who God is. One seminary professor said, "People seek out new gods the way they seek out new products in the marketplace." How would you describe God?

1. The first two of the Ten Commandments say there is but one God and no others. More than anything else, we need to get this right. God gets angry about our worshiping false, man-made gods.
2. The best way to define God is through a man—Jesus. He is God's ultimate revelation of Himself.

How do you understand Jesus? The most authoritative word is the Bible. Scripture gives us the complete and full picture of Jesus. Otherwise, it's just somebody's opinion.

How do you define God? Get to know the Jesus of Scripture.

I promise, you will not be disappointed.

HEART CONDITION

> *"... TODAY IF YOU HEAR HIS VOICE,*
> *DO NOT HARDEN YOUR HEARTS ..."*
> **—Hebrews 3:15**

I once read about a head coach in the NBA who drifted from God. He was dabbling in Buddhism, Zen, and other different things. He told a reporter that when he went back to his father's church, at times it felt like the preacher was preaching directly at him with a message about the need to repent and to be saved through Jesus Christ.

The reporter asked, "Well, how did you respond?"

He said, "Well, I just hardened my heart until the service was over."

I cringed when I read that. It's such an honest, graphic description of how the majority of the world responds to the Good News of Jesus Christ. Many just harden their hearts one more time because they're more interested in doing their own thing than in following God. But the Bible tells us, "Today if you hear His voice, do not harden your hearts."

I urge you, don't harden your heart again. Instead, choose to trust Christ and follow Him today and forevermore.

March 20

SIGNS OF JESUS' RETURN

"But of that day and hour no one knows . . ."
—Matthew 24:36

One of the teachings of Jesus is that He will come again. He very clearly teaches about signs of His coming:

An increase in false teachers and messiahs. False teaching is contrary to God's written word; we see this today not only in cults, but also inside and outside the church.

Wars and rumors of wars. The twentieth century was the bloodiest and worst century in all history. What will the twenty-first century hold?

Increase in natural disasters. Earthquakes, tsunamis, hurricanes, famines, and floods.

He says these occurrences are like birth pangs. With the onset of labor, birth pangs increase in frequency and intensity as birth approaches. This is very revealing in reflecting on the "signs" of which Jesus speaks.

Yet He clearly states, "No one knows the time." If someone sets a time, you can be sure he is a false prophet because no one knows the time. We need to be ready *all the time*. One thing is for sure, however, birth pangs keep increasing.

March 21

THE FACTS VS. THE TRUTH IN GOSSIP

". . . he who spreads slander is a fool."
—Proverbs 10:18

A pastor went to visit a woman from his church before she was to have serious surgery. As he walked into her hospital room, he found her in the arms of a man who was not her husband. Stunned and embarrassed, he silently walked out. Later he discovered that this woman's brother had flown in from California to comfort her before her surgery.

Later, the pastor said, "I could have told others I saw that woman in the arms of a man who was not her husband and it would have been a fact, but it would not have been the truth."

The press often does this in reporting what people have done. They confuse the facts with the truth. This results in half-truths that are really the worst forms of lies, because they are so believable. Gossip and slander are big on facts and short on truth. They unfairly destroy people's character.

The next time you hear something bad about another person, be sure you have more than the facts. Be sure you have the whole truth, for it is easy to confuse the facts with the truth.

The Future

"Now may the God of hope fill you with all joy
and peace in believing . . ."
—Romans 15:13

What's going to happen next year, next week, fifteen minutes from now? Many people waste time worrying about what might happen. The Bible gives us a wonderful promise: "[God says] I know the plans I have for you, plans to prosper you and not to harm you, plans to give you a hope and a future."

Can we know the future? No, we can't. But we can face the future with confidence when we know God is in control and is working for our good.

No matter what circumstances come our way, we know He's there for us. And frankly, when I read the newspapers or see the evening news, I don't always feel optimistic about the future. But when I put my trust in God, knowing He is in complete control, I have hope for tomorrow and strength for living each and every day.

A LIFE WELL SPENT

"An inheritance gained hurriedly at the beginning will not be blessed in the end."
—Proverbs 20:21

The track record on second and third generation wealth is a disaster. That famous philosopher, Anonymous, once wrote, "The best way to create a small fortune is to inherit a large one." The Bible tells us it's good to leave an inheritance to our children—but if we focus our inheritance only on money and material possessions, that's a problem.

In the book, *A Life Well Spent*, Russ Crosson wrote that our primary focus should be on posterity, not prosperity. When it comes to our heirs, we need to invest in their lives, help them build faith and character, teach them hard work, and how to handle money wisely. If all the focus of our inheritance is on prosperity, our posterity will be severely handicapped when it comes to faith, responsibility, generosity, and character.

We want to help our children become producers, more than consumers. That calls for a lot of love, time, and most of all, a great example.

Parents, when it comes to inheritance, what are you going to leave your children? Let's leave an inheritance more valuable than money.

March 24

OVERCOMING REJECTION

"Do not be overcome by evil, but overcome evil with good."
—Romans 12:21

Rejection is never easy, but rejection from people we care about really hurts. Maybe it's the rejection of losing your job or having a spouse walk out on you. Sometimes rejection can be so devastating we're not sure we are going to recover. Here are a few thoughts that may help.

Jesus understands. On the cross, He faced the rejection of the whole world. Be honest with God about your feelings. He understands.

Don't seek revenge. Trust God to bring about ultimate justice. Ask God to help you forgive. After all, Jesus forgave us for rejecting Him on the cross.

Don't confuse forgiveness with a lack of accountability. Holding wrong-doers accountable is good—for them, for us, and for others.

Choose to get better, not bitter. The best way to get even in a good way is to get better. Remember, "Bitterness is the poison we swallow while hoping the other person dies."

These four insights can help you overcome rejection. Put them into practice and rejection will not defeat you. Rejection is never easy, but overcoming rejection is a key to successful living.

March 25

HOPE

"This hope we have as an anchor of the soul,
a hope both sure and steadfast . . ."
—Hebrews 6:19

There's an old saying: "When a person loses hope, they begin to hope for death." Life is hard without hope. Life becomes drudgery, misery, meaningless. One reason people lose hope is that they put their hope in the wrong things—beliefs that disappoint, dreams that are unrealistic, but, most of all, in other people who disappoint and disillusion us about life and, sadly, even about God.

But God never disappoints. He gets blamed for a lot of evil that people do, but He is the one we want to put our hope in. He always wants the best for us. His Word says, "I know the plans I have for you, to give you hope and a future." He always loves us. He's always faithful. Even in death He gives us hope. In His son Jesus, we see He understands the pain of death and He gives us the hope of victory over death as well. When we have hope over death, we can begin to live hopefully every day.

March 26

AN OUTRAGEOUS CLAIM

". . . I did not come to abolish, but to fulfill."
—Matthew 5:17

One of the most outrageous claims ever made by a man was this: "Do you think I have come to abolish the law or the prophets? I have not come to abolish them but to fulfill them."

The man who made that claim was Jesus and the law and the prophets He referred to was Scripture. Jesus claimed to be the fulfillment of how to live a good and moral life. He claimed to be the fulfillment of the prophets of old like Isaiah, Jeremiah, and Daniel. Wow! What a claim!

He showed this through His life, His death, and His resurrection from the dead. To believe Scripture is to believe Jesus. To believe Jesus is to believe He fulfills the Scripture. But even more, He shows us how to fulfill the commands of God.

When asked what the greatest commandment was He replied, "Love the Lord your God with your heart, soul, and mind and your neighbor as yourself." You can't obey one without the other. Jesus is the only one to perfectly fulfill God's Word.

March 27

SECULARISM

"No man can by any means redeem his brother
or give to God a ransom for him . . ."
—Psalm 49:7

Secularism may be the fastest growing religion in America today. The National Opinion Research Center at the University of Chicago found that those who aren't affiliated with a religion rose from nine percent in 1993 to fourteen percent in 2002. Twenty-seven percent of those born after 1980 had no religious affiliation.

What is secularism? It's the view that man, not God, is the ultimate authority and that consideration of the present well-being of mankind should predominate over religious considerations in civil affairs and public education.

Secularism is all about man. Yet, here's the irony—secularism leads to disillusionment with man and hopelessness at death. But Christianity is all about God and His desire to redeem sinful man through Christ. Christianity's worldview leads us to understand that man only finds ultimate meaning in how he relates to God. It is realistic, yet filled with hope.

March 28

THE GREAT WALL

"Who will separate us from the love of Christ?
Will tribulation, or distress, or persecution, or famine,
or nakedness, or peril, or sword?"
—Romans 8:35

In January 2000, I had the privilege of seeing the Great Wall of China. It was magnificent. Construction began over four hundred years before Christ and was completed in the 1600's. It's built over some of the toughest terrain imaginable. You could stretch it from Atlanta to London and still have wall left over. All that effort to stay separated from their enemies.

As big as the Great Wall is, it's not as big as the wall of sin that separates man from God. I know sin is not a politically correct term these days, but it's what separates us from God. No man can overcome this barrier on his own. Yet God offers us a way through Jesus, His sacrificial death, and our faith in Him. He removes the barrier.

Do you feel a barrier or separation between you and God? Look in faith at what God's Word says about Jesus. He'll remove the wall between you and God.

March 29

Jesus and Scripture

"... if you knew Me, you would know My Father also."
—John 8:19

Who is history's most influential person?

I believe it's Jesus Christ. Every time we write the date, it's a testimony to Him. But it's important to remember that we are directly dependent on Scripture to give us the full view of Jesus. To know Jesus we need to know Scripture. Jesus said, "Do not think I came to abolish the law or the prophets. I did not come to abolish but to fulfill." All Scripture, from Moses and the Old Testament prophets, to the gospels and the writings of Paul and John's Revelation, reveals Jesus to us.

If we ignore Scripture, we will not know Jesus. When we choose what we like and ignore what we don't, we get a distorted view of Jesus. We get a man-made, politically correct Jesus who is not Jesus at all. Scripture reveals the true Jesus. Jesus reveals God to us. Get to know Jesus and you get to know God.

March 30

LEGALISM

"There shall be one standard for you . . . for I am the LORD your God."
—**Leviticus 24:22**

Legalism is not true faith. It's often confused with dedicated faith, but real faith is not about obeying well-intentioned, man-made rules. That only leads to frustration, resentment, and unnecessary guilt. In today's world, there are not only religious legalists but secular legalists. The tolerance police and politically correct Gestapo are intensely passionate about enforcing their well-intentioned man-made rules. Resentment and frustration result.

If you suffer from well-intentioned legalism, I have great news for you. Jesus battled legalism throughout His ministry. He understands your pain. He wants to save you from it, just as He wants to save you from sin.

He will clarify what God calls sin and give you the desire to obey Him. God's commands enrich our lives. Man's legalisms enslave our lives. The only way to know the difference is by looking to Christ through God's Word. You'll discover the truth and the truth will set you free.

The Biggest Fool

"... You fool! This very night your soul is required of you; and now who will own what you have prepared?"
—Luke 12:20

Jesus Christ tells of the biggest fool. "A certain rich man was very productive and he thought to himself, 'What shall I do since I have no place to store all that I have?' He decided to tear down his barns and build larger ones and then store all his grain and goods. Then he said, 'I have many goods laid up for years to come; now I'll take it easy and eat, drink, and be merry!'

"But God said to him, 'You fool! This very night your life is required of you and now who will own all that you have?' So is the man who lays up treasure for himself, and is not rich toward God."

Question: When are you going to pause long enough from pursuing bigger barns and dreaming of how to fill them up, to start thinking about your soul? All that counts is "Do you know God?" and "What have you done for God and your fellow man?" Quit playing the fool and get things right with God through Jesus Christ. And do it today!

April 1

FOOLS

"In all your ways acknowledge Him,
and He will make your paths straight."
—Proverbs 3:6

You make a fool of yourself when you argue with an ass. The Bible tells of a man named Balaam in Numbers 22. He was headed in the wrong direction. He wanted to please himself and was ignoring God, so God spoke to him through his donkey. Balaam was furiously mad at the animal! He argued with it and almost beat it to death until he realized that God was seeking to speak to him, to help him get on the right path.

Sometimes God goes to extraordinary means to get our attention when we are hellbent on going our own self-destructive ways. It could come through a financial jolt or through a rebellious child. When those times come, getting angry may be foolish, but taking time to listen may be the key to seeking God's guidance about the right way to go.

Is God trying to get your attention to keep you from making a fool of yourself? Take time to listen and He'll change your course and get you where you need to go.

April 2

AMERICA SEEKING SPIRITUALITY

"I am the Lord your God . . .
You shall have no other gods before Me."
—Exodus 20:2–3

Have you noticed a certain irony in America? While America is becoming more and more secular, it is also becoming more spiritual. While America seems more and more godless, it is also becoming a land of many gods. As people recognize that there must be some higher power in life, they still rebel against the idea of any authority over their personal lives. People want spirituality their own way, with no strings attached. But the spiritual pursuits of all these man-made gods is a dead end.

Hint: There is only one true way to God, and that is through Jesus Christ. He said that Himself in the most controversial statement He made: "I am the way, and the truth, and the life; no one comes to the Father but through Me."

Don't fall into the indecisive patterns of the majority. Look to Jesus Christ and find the answer to what you've been missing: the way to God, true spirituality.

April 3

JESUS, THE LIGHT
THAT OVERCOMES DARKNESS

"I have come as light into the world,
that everyone who believes in Me may not remain in darkness."
—John 12:46

Have you ever been in a situation where the darkness was so powerful that light could not overcome it? I remember touring a cave when all the lights were turned off. I couldn't see a thing. I couldn't see my hand in front of my face! And then the guide simply lit a match—one match—and we could see all over the cave, because darkness cannot overcome the light.

Jesus says He is the light of the world, the embodiment of how to know God and how to live life. You may feel your life is engulfed in darkness. You may feel bewildered at not having discovered the answer to life. Invite Christ into your life and the light will be turned on, no matter how much darkness you've experienced. Life will begin to make sense and you'll be filled with hope and understanding.

Here's more good news. When we do this, Jesus says we can be a light to others by pointing people who are in the dark to the light—the light of Christ.

April 4

MONEY ... SLAVE OR MASTER

"... It is more blessed to give than receive."
—Acts 20:35

In the book *Days of Grace*, Arthur Ashe shares his philosophy about money. He says, "From what we get, we can make a living; what we give, however, makes a life." What a great perspective on money. The focus is on giving rather than on getting, and that makes all the difference.

As long as our focus is on getting all we can, canning all we get, and sitting on that can, we're slaves to our money. Our happiness depends on how much we have. On the other hand, when we view money as a tool for accomplishing good, it becomes our servant. That attitude frees us to use money as God intended—to provide for our needs, but also to do good for others.

Jesus addresses the bottom line: "You cannot serve God and money." How about it? Are you the master of your money, or is your money your master? Master or slave? The choice is yours.

WEATHER ALERT

"But seeing the wind, he became afraid, and beginning to sink,
he cried out, saying, 'Lord, save me!'"
—Matthew 14:30

Life is filled with storms. It may be smooth sailing for a while, and then suddenly a storm comes. The boss informs you that you no longer have a job; your spouse files for divorce, or the doctor says those dreaded words, "You have cancer."

Jesus appeared to His disciples when they were at sea in a storm. Because He was walking on water, Peter said, "Lord, if it's You, command me to walk in the water with You." He did and Peter stepped out of the boat in faith. He was doing OK as long as He focused on Jesus. But suddenly, he thought about what he was doing and looked at the darkness of the sea. Amidst the howling winds, he was overcome with fear and began to sink. At the last moment, he cried out to Jesus to save him and Jesus did.

Taking his eyes off Jesus and focusing on the dangers of the storm overwhelmed Peter. But God is bigger than any storm. Focus on Him in faith and He'll give you the strength to get through the storms of life victoriously.

April 6

Waiting on God

"Rest in the Lord and wait patiently for Him . . ."
—Psalm 37:7

I don't like to wait in long lines at restaurants, being stuck in traffic during rush hour, or being put on hold by a computer. Waiting is a waste of time. This is why waiting on God is so difficult for many believers. That's also why many people quote the verse that is *not* in the Bible, "God helps those who help themselves." That's American ideology, but it's not biblical.

The statement speaks to lack of faith, how God needs us to take charge to get things done. But one thing's for sure: What we need to do is to trust God and be willing to do His will, in His timing, not our own, for the right action at the right time equals the right result.

Waiting on God is tough, but God's timing is always best for us and for others.

April 7

Parenting Teens

"Likewise, urge the young men to be sensible;"
—Titus 2:6

Parenting preschoolers and children is physically and emotionally demanding, but nothing is more emotionally demanding than parenting teens. Peer pressure, their desire for freedom, and your desire to not let go too fast can cause all kinds of stress. A few thoughts:

If you've taught them to obey at six, there's a better chance they'll obey at sixteen.

If you take time to listen to them when they're young, there's a better chance they'll listen to you as a teenager.

Don't sweat the generational differences. Instead, ask these questions:

1. Is what they are doing unbiblical?
2. Have they defied me?
3. Will it bring them harm?

If the answer to any of these is "yes," it's time for discipline and instruction with a good dose of love.

Pray that they will desire to make decisions that are pleasing to God, for when they do, you'll never have to worry about them pleasing you. This is more important than their happiness, for this is true joy.

April 8

SAUL TO PAUL

But the Lord said to [Ananias], "Go, for [Saul] is a chosen instrument of Mine, to bear My name before the Gentiles and kings and the sons of Israel;"
—Acts 9:15

He was the worst kind of terrorist—a religious terrorist—plotting to kill and hurt people who didn't believe in God like he did. He was brilliant, highly educated, and ambitious. The mention of his name would strike fear in people who didn't believe as he did.

One day on his way to fulfill another terrorist plot, he was stopped by a power he didn't know existed. It terrified him. This person was so powerful that the young terrorist stopped in his tracks. The terrorist was named Saul. The powerful person was Jesus.

On that day, the terrorist named Saul was changed inwardly and outwardly by the love of Christ. Christ changed his name to Paul and God used Paul to be the greatest theologian and missionary in the history of the church. Christ can change anyone who is hostile to Him and His church—even religious terrorists. He can even change people who are sinners like you and me.

I Am the Resurrection and the Life

"I am the resurrection and the life;
he who believes in Me shall live even if he dies,
and everyone who lives and believes in Me shall never die."
—John 11:25–26

One of the more outrageous claims of Jesus was, "I am the resurrection and the life. He who believes in Me will live, even if he dies, and everyone who lives and believes in Me will never die." He concluded this claim by asking the crowd, "Do you believe this?"

How would you have responded?

Jesus was claiming to have power over death. He was claiming that He was the source of eternal life. He was claiming that even if a person dies physically and they believe in Him, they will never die spiritually. Do you believe this?

How you answer Jesus' question concerning His claims about Himself and power over death is the most important decision you'll ever make. Let's put it this way: if He didn't rise from the dead, the decision is easy. Don't believe Him. But if He did, we have an important decision to make—a decision of life and death.

I believe Him. How about you?

April 10

PRIDE

"Pride goes before destruction,
and a haughty spirit before stumbling."
—**Proverbs 16:18**

It was a spring day, April 10 to be exact, and it seemed that all of South Hampton, England, had gathered in one place to celebrate one of the pinnacle accomplishments of man. About 2,200 people had the privilege of a first-hand view, among them some of the wealthiest people in the world. It seemed the whole world was marveling at this awesome accomplishment: eleven stories high, 900 feet long, 46,000 tons. Yet just five days later, at 2:20 a.m. on April 15, 1912, it was all gone—disappeared—a massive wreckage at the bottom of the sea. The name *Titanic* was always preceded by the word "unsinkable." On board, many joked, "Even God couldn't sink the *Titanic*," but it will forever serve as the twentieth century example of the foolishness of pride.

God's Word says, "Pride goes before a fall, and a haughty spirit before stumbling." Prideful *Titanics* sink into destruction, but a good life that is humble before God and man has a better chance to withstand the storms of life.

April 11

MARY MAGDALENE

"Now after He had risen early on the first day of the week,
He first appeared to Mary Magdalene . . ."
—Mark 16:9

The best seller, *The DaVinci Code,* has made Mary Magdalene a hot topic of discussion. Who was she? Was she Jesus' wife and the mother of His child as the book claims? Or was she simply a dedicated follower of Jesus?

She is an important person in the story of Jesus because she was one of the women who went to anoint the body of Jesus after His death. That was the custom in those days. But the tomb was empty. And while Mary was bewildered at this, Jesus appeared to her *alive.* His first appearance after His resurrection was to a woman.

Jesus took women seriously in that patriarchal first-century world. He did more to raise the status of women than anyone who has ever lived. But there is no historical evidence or documentation that Mary Magdalene was Jesus' wife. That is pure fantasy. She is simply a good example of what it means to be a devoted follower of Jesus.

April 12

JESUS MAKING RELIGIOUS PEOPLE MAD

"And God said . . . I AM WHO I AM."
—**Exodus 3:14**

Jesus was constantly making religious people mad. What made them the angriest were His claims about Himself. He said, "I *am* the bread of life," and "I *am* the light of this world," meaning enlightenment. He said, "I *am* the way," meaning the way to God. He said, "I *am* the truth." "I *am* the life," meaning the key to eternal life. He said, "Before Abraham was, I AM."

These are definite claims to be God. These were outrageous statements and were the major reason that Jesus was executed. The religious people saw Him as a blasphemer, a pretender who claimed to be God.

Whatever you do, don't commit intellectual suicide by claiming you think Jesus was a good man, a prophet, a good teacher, but not God. Our only rational conclusions can be that He was an idiot, a lying megalomaniac, or He is who He claimed to be. I believe He told the truth about Himself.

What do you believe?

April 13

REAL SOUL FOOD

*"I am the living bread that came down out of heaven; if anyone
eats of this bread, he shall live foreve;"*
—John 6:51

Some of my most satisfying times are spent enjoying good soul food
with close friends and family: fried chicken, turnip greens, mashed
potatoes, macaroni and cheese, cornbread, and butter beans. Man, it
makes my mouth water just thinking about it.

But the ultimate soul food is the Bread of Life. Have you tasted this
bread? This food makes you feel satisfied and content, sort of like your
favorite meal. But only the Bread of Life provides *lasting* satisfaction and
contentment. Jesus tells us He is the Bread of Life, the ultimate soul food,
because only He provides us with spiritual nourishment that lasts.

During the Passover meal the night before His crucifixion, He
broke bread with the disciples. He said the bread symbolized His body
and that He would be broken on the cross. Christ wanted all of us to
know He is the Bread of Life: the only food that brings contentment
and fulfillment to our souls.

I love soul food, especially the ultimate soul food, the Bread of
Life—Jesus Christ.

Life's Most Important Question

"Pilate said to them, 'Then what shall I do with Jesus who is called Christ?'"
—**Matthew 27:22**

Almost 2,000 years ago, a man named Pilate asked the most important question in life. Standing before him was an itinerant preacher. There was nothing remarkable about His looks. He had attracted a large following, but had few committed followers. He had no wealth, not even a home of His own. Yet He was the object of unmitigated hatred from a mob. Pilate asked, "What shall I do with this man?" As the mob cried for His execution, the man, Jesus Christ, stood silently as Pilate cowardly sentenced Him to death on the cross.

The question Pilate asked is ultimately one all of us have to ask: "What shall I do with this man Jesus?"

He loves you, even when you couldn't care less about Him. He cared enough to pay the penalty for your sin. What will you do with Jesus? Your eternal destiny hangs in the balance by how you respond.

April 15

Do You Believe He Is Risen?

"He is not here, for He has risen, just as He said."
—Matthew 28:6

On the first Easter morning, a group of women went to the tomb to anoint the body of Jesus. There was no doubt in their minds Jesus was dead. They saw Him die on Friday and they even saw where He was buried. Yet, when they arrived on Easter, the tomb was empty. They were alarmed.

Can you imagine how you would feel if you took flowers to the grave of a loved one two days after the funeral, and the grave had been dug up, the casket was open, and the body was gone? Terrifying! But an angel said to them, "He is not here. He is risen." The angel reminded them that Christ preached that He would be killed and rise again. The women believed. How about you?

If Christ did not rise from the dead, He was a fraud or a looney-tune and certainly not a great prophet or teacher. Or, He did what He said He'd do—conquer death—which makes Him God.

What do you believe? All of Christianity rises and falls on the resurrection.

Hope at Easter

"And the angel . . . said to the women, 'Do not be afraid;
for I know that you are looking for Jesus who has been crucified.
He is not here, for He has risen, just as He said.'"
—Matthew 28:5–6

When we lose a loved one, we want the whole world to stop and take notice. The world, however, keeps rushing on and darkness can engulf our soul.

A Christian man lost his eighteen-year-old son. It was a tragic death and the father felt his soul engulfed in darkness. Easter came and he dreaded the day. He arose early, unable to sleep. He sat alone in the darkness of his home. He felt the darkness of his son's death mocking his soul on a day when in the past he had always felt such hope. Then he saw the sun rise.

As he watched it rise and bring light to another day, he heard the *Hallelujah Chorus* being sung over the radio. At that moment he felt God speaking to him, saying, "As the sun rises, my Son rose and so will yours."

The man realized there will be no darkness in heaven—only light. There will be no death—only life—because Jesus is risen indeed! This is why Easter is such a glorious day.

April 17

WHEN CHRISTIANITY IS WORTHLESS

"But if there is no resurrection of the dead,
then not even Christ has been raised;"
—1 Corinthians 15:13

Do you know what would make Christianity worthless?
If Christ did not rise from the dead, Christianity would be built around a big lie. It would mean Jesus was a liar, because He said He would be killed and rise again. It would mean that the Bible is filled with lies, because over and over it writes of Jesus' resurrection. It would mean that of all people on earth, Christians are to be pitied the most, for we have bought into a colossal hoax.

But if Christ rose from the dead, it means that when Jesus says He is the Son of God, He is believable. It means there is hope beyond the grave. It means every miracle in the Bible is believable. After all, if a man rises from the dead, what's the big deal about parting the Red Sea or making the lame walk? Christianity rises and falls on the resurrection. No resurrection, and Christianity is worthless. But if He did rise, it means everything.

I believe He did. How about you?

April 18

Why I Believe in God

"Now the centurion, and those who were with him keeping guard over Jesus . . . said, 'Truly this was the Son of God.'"
—**Matthew 27:54**

The big reason I believe in God is the overwhelming evidence of Jesus' resurrection from the dead. If He didn't, He wasn't God. But if He did, well, men like Mohammed and Buddha just don't compare. Have you examined the overwhelming evidence of Jesus' resurrection?

All the authorities had to do was produce His body, and Christianity was dead on arrival. No one did.

In fear, all the disciples deserted Jesus at His crucifixion; yet, they went from being cowards to courageously proclaiming His resurrection. They died martyrs' deaths for refusing to stop telling what they knew to be true.

Some said the disciples stole the body and lied about His resurrection to start a new movement. But hold on. People will die for a lie *if they don't know it's a lie,* but people don't die for a lie they know *is* a lie. Someone would have squealed.

So much evidence and yet there is so much more. The overwhelming evidence of Jesus' resurrection is the number one reason I believe in God.

April 19

MANY LIVE APPEARANCES AFTER HIS DEATH

". . . because I live, you shall live also."
—John 14:19

Christianity is about faith—faith in Jesus Christ who rose from the dead. But have you realized there is also historical documentation of Jesus' resurrection? Six different books of the Bible offer documentation of Jesus' nine live appearances after His resurrection:

1. He appeared to Mary Magdalene and other women the morning of His resurrection.
2. He appeared to Peter.
3. He appeared to two men on the road to Emmaus.
4. He appeared to the disciples as a whole (except for Thomas, who wasn't there).
5. He appeared to the disciples with Thomas, and Thomas believed.
6. He appeared to seven disciples at the Sea of Galilee and enjoyed a fish fry.
7. He appeared to over 500 people at once.
8. He appeared to James, his brother.
9. He appeared one final time to His disciples before He ascended to heaven.

There are at least nine documented live appearances after His death. That is a lot of evidence that He rose from the dead.

April 20

SWOON THEORY

"He is not here, but He has risen."
—Luke 24:6

We've been looking at the resurrection of Jesus Christ and the many theories espoused to debunk it. Let me share with you one of the funniest theories that tries to explain the empty tomb. It's called the swoon theory.

This theory argues that Jesus really didn't die. The Roman guards just *thought* He had died, but he was really unconscious or had swooned from the loss of blood and exhaustion on the cross. Later He revived and came out of the tomb and appeared to His disciples, who thought He had risen.

Yeah, sure. After the ordeal of the crucifixion in losing all His blood, He survived three days in a damp tomb without food or water, unwrapped Himself from tightly bound burial clothes, rolled away the heavy stone, overcame the Roman guards, walked miles on feet that had been spiked, and convinced His disciples He had risen from the dead. It takes more faith to believe this theory than to believe in the Resurrection.

In the end, the only theory that explains the empty tomb is Jesus' resurrection from the dead, and that's the evidence I believe.

April 21

More Thoughts on the Resurrection

"You are witnesses of these things."
—Luke 24:48

One of the major questions people ask when considering the resurrection of Jesus is how to explain the dramatic change in the disciples. Consider the following:

At His crucifixion, all but one fled in fear and they went into hiding—for as His followers, they feared government authorities would arrest them as well. Later, in different parts of the world, they boldly proclaimed that Jesus had risen from the dead. When confronted with death if they didn't stop making that claim, none did. People will die for a lie that they don't know is a lie, but they don't die for something that they know is a hoax. Someone would have squealed and no one did. Why?

That first Easter morning when the women told the disciples that Jesus was risen, the disciples did not believe them. They thought it was nonsense. They knew He was dead. What happened to cause them to believe He was alive?

Can you answer these questions? I believe Jesus arose, and they saw Him, and their lives were never the same.

April 22

THE EMPTY TOMB

". . . and if Christ has not been raised, then our preaching is vain, your faith also is vain."
—1 Corinthians 15:14

If you're a skeptic about the resurrection of Jesus, how do you explain the empty tomb? Some say the disciples stole the body. Matthew 28:11–15 speaks of this rumor.

I ask: how could they overcome the Roman guards, who would be executed if they left their post or lost their prisoner? And how can you explain all the disciples dying a martyr's death at different locations and times for proclaiming something they knew to be a lie?

People will die for a lie if they don't know it's a lie, but people don't die for something they know is untrue. Do you remember Watergate and all those Nixon loyalists running for their lawyers when they realized prison might be ahead?

The disciples claimed that Jesus Christ proved He was God's son by rising from the dead. To escape martyrdom, all the disciples had to do was renounce their claim. They did not.

No, the disciples didn't steal Jesus' body. They died because they knew that Jesus rose.

Winning the Race

"What is this confidence that you have? We trust in the Lord our God. . . ."
—2 Kings 18:19, 22

During the filming of the old classic movie, *Ben Hur,* Charleton Heston had a terrible time learning to drive the chariot. When it came time to film the key sequence of the chariot race, Heston told the director, "I think I can drive the chariot, but I don't think I can win the race." The director replied, "You just drive, and I'll see to it that you win."

Wouldn't it be great if we could be assured of victory in life? Wouldn't we like to know that, even though the circumstances don't always seem to be in our favor, the ultimate outcome would be positive?

I have good news for you. This principle does hold true. Those who place their trust in Jesus Christ, who seek to follow His guidance and direction for living, can be sure of ultimate victory through eternal life. Live life God's way. He assures the victory.

April 24

WORK TO THE GLORY OF GOD

"For God is not unjust so as to forget your work and the love
which you have shown toward His name . . ."
—Hebrews 6:10

The story is told of a woman who cleaned the same office building for many years. When asked how she endured the drudgery of doing the same chores day in and day out, she replied, "It's not drudgery. You see, I'm working for the King and He's pleased along with others when I do my best."

This woman found the secret to satisfying work. Her focus was not on the tasks, but on the Lord and people. She focused on serving the Lord and her fellow man. How about you? When was the last time you found joy in your work?

The Bible gives us a key: "Whatever you do . . . do all for the glory of God." When we work for the Lord and to serve other people, work can bring us joy and fulfillment. It all depends on our attitude.

Are you anticipating another day of drudgery? That's what you'll probably get. But if you're planning to live this day to please God and to serve others, you may be surprised how the drudgery is replaced by meaning and purpose.

April 25

Hooking Up

". . . the body is not for immorality, but for the Lord;"
—1 Corinthians 6:13

In Tom Wolfe's book, *Hooking Up,* he writes, "Sexual revolution was a rather prim term for the lurid carnival actually taking place in the mightiest country on earth . . . an estimated 50% of all [Web] hits were at sites purveying what was known as 'adult material.'"

In the year 2000, hooking up was a term known to almost every American child over the age of nine, but to only a relatively small percentage of their parents, who thought it was used in the old sense of meeting someone. Children knew hooking up meant having a sexual experience.

No doubt, America's sexual standards are not what God had in mind when He invented sex. Sex is His idea, but for only one setting—in the context of marriage between a man and a woman. It's difficult to live by, and is radically counter-cultural, but God loves you and wants the best for you. Do you have the courage to trust Him in this and every area of your life? You won't be disappointed.

April 26

You Can't Take It with You

*"For we have brought nothing into the world,
so we cannot take anything out of it either."*
—1 Timothy 6:7

I've been a pastor for many years, and have attended a lot of funerals. But I've never seen a moving van following the hearse.

Think about the priorities and interests of your life. How much time is spent acquiring and hoarding things you simply can't take with you? The Bible states that we have brought nothing into the world, so we cannot take any stuff out of it either. It's good to focus on the things that last—like God and building eternal treasure.

THERMOMETER OR THERMOSTAT?

"And who is the one who overcomes the world,
but he who believes that Jesus is the Son of God."
—1 John 5:5

Have you ever thought about the difference between a thermometer and a thermostat? A thermometer changes with circumstances—it reacts. A thermostat changes the circumstances—it regulates.

The same could be said for the way people respond to life's challenges. Some let circumstances control them and they often feel like victims. But others experience life on a more even keel. Circumstances may become difficult, but they're constantly overcoming those difficult circumstances. They weather the storms with the confidence that circumstances have no power to defeat them.

Which are you? A thermometer—constantly up and down? Or a thermostat—strong and unshakeable?

I find that people who have a strong personal relationship with Jesus Christ experience great strength and inner peace no matter what their circumstances. They don't see themselves as victims, but always as overcomers. It's a real key to successful living.

PRUNING

"... every branch that bears fruit, He prunes it,
that it may bear more fruit."
—John 15:2

Are you a gardener? Do you enjoy seeing things grow? If so, you understand the principle that a plant must be pruned to produce at its peak. Dead wood and unhealthy parts must be cut away.

Pruning is a reality in the garden, but it's also a very real part of human life. Because God loves us, sometimes He chooses to prune our lives. This may come through the loss of a job or a loved one, or a move away from something that's comfortable for us. It may happen in many ways when we face adversity.

What is accomplished by pruning? For the plant, it's a healthier and more vigorous growth with more fruit. For us, it's the ability to rely more completely on God, our source of life, and the ability to live a more spiritually secure and disciplined life.

Pruning is painful; but it allows us to live a more fruitful life. With God, pruning always gives us hope.

April 29

JUDGING OTHERS

*"And why do you look at the speck that is in your brother's eye,
but do not notice the log that is in your own eye?"*
—Matthew 7:3

Imagine that you need surgery to remove a splinter of wood from your eye. It's a dangerous procedure; one slip of the scalpel and you are ruined. The doctor tells you that the surgery will be no problem, but something about the doctor is so horrifying it's comical. You notice he has a two-by-four through both his eyes.

That ludicrous scene is what Jesus was illustrating when He talked about judging others. He said, "Do not judge or you too will be judged . . . Why do you look at the speck of sawdust in your brother's eye, and pay no attention to the plank in your own eye . . . you hypocrite? First take the plank out of your own eye, and then you will see clearly to remove the speck from your brother's eye."

In judging the flaws of others, we are often blind to our own. It's ludicrous to get in the judging business, for none of us has good enough vision to know the whole story. Only God sees with complete vision. He's the only one with 20/20 vision in understanding another person's life. Let's get into the loving business and leave the judging to God.

April 30

A Word about Worship

"Come, let us worship and bow down;"
—Psalm 95:6

Worship is the number one ministry priority in our church. We hope and pray that the weekend worship will be the most exciting and meaningful event of each person's week, a place for Christians to get their spiritual batteries charged, and a place for seekers to find God.

Soren Kierkegaard, a Danish philosopher in the nineteenth century, once clarified the most common misconception about worship using the analogy of a drama. "When we come to worship God, we generally feel as though the preacher and other ministers are the performers and God is the subject of the performance and we as the congregation are merely the audience . . . but this is a terrible misunderstanding of worship."

Kierkegaard is describing a consumer-oriented approach, focused more on what we receive than what we give. Kierkegaard goes on to say, "Authentic Christian worship is just the opposite. We, the congregation, are the performers. The preachers and other ministers are the directors of the performance and God is the audience."

Next time you worship, try this perspective. It just might make it a more meaningful experience.

May 1

THE TRUTH

"Jesus answered . . . 'Everyone who is of the truth
hears My voice.'"
—**John 18:37**

In the spring of 2001, the collision of an American spy plane and a Chinese fighter jet caused both governments to blame each other. Two governments, two nations, but each had completely different views of the truth. By the very definition of truth, both could not be right. Yet many people from every religious persuasion have embraced universalism: the idea that every religion is equally valid and all men can get to God and heaven their own way.

Consider what Jesus said: "I am the way, the truth, the life. No one comes to the Father but through Me." If all religions are a valid way to God, then Jesus was not telling the truth. And if Jesus was not telling the truth, He is not the only way. Truth, by definition, means that one statement is true and a contradicting statement is false.

Either Jesus is truth or universalism is truth. What do you believe? I believe Jesus.

May 2

TRUTH OR CONSEQUENCES

"If we confess our sins, He is faithful and righteous to forgive us our sins and to cleanse us from all unrighteousness."
—1 John 1:9

There was a game show in the early days of television called *Truth Or Consequences*. Contestants had to answer questions correctly or face embarrassing consequences.

The Bible is a book of truth and consequences; it tells the truth about God and how to live. It also makes the consequences of ignoring God's teaching very clear. In the Bible, we read the stories of people who failed to obey God's guidelines and the tragic results of their failure to do so.

We also read that God provided a way for all of us to escape the inevitable consequences of sin. Jesus Christ, through His perfect life and sacrificial death, paid the price for our sin. He will not remove the consequences of wrongdoing here on earth, but He does forgive us and removes the eternal consequences of our sin.

The big question for your life is, "Will you believe the truth, or face the consequences?" The decision is yours.

Soul Mate

"Two are better than one . . ."
—Ecclesiastes 4:9

Everyone is looking for a soul mate—someone you really click with, a person who enriches your life while you enrich his or hers.

The term has a basis in the very first marriage. The first time God said something was "not good" had to do with Adam being alone. God's ideal is for each man and woman to have their spouse as their soul mate, a person of the opposite sex who is a perfect complement.

God was the first anesthesiologist and put Adam to sleep. He was the first surgeon when He removed a rib. He was the first master artist as He formed that rib into a woman, the first matchmaker, and first Father of the bride. He brought Eve to Adam. Adam was thrilled and said, "Bone of my bone, flesh of my flesh. She shall be called Woman." In the Bible, the word for body means soul.

Is your spouse your soul mate? It's what God has in mind for your marriage. The first marriage shows it, and in Christ, God gives us the power to experience it in our own marriages.

May 4

THE ANTICHRIST

"Who is the liar but the one who denies that Jesus is the Christ?
This is the antichrist,
the one who denies the Father and the Son."
—1 John 2:22

In your opinion, who's the greatest communicator—past or present? Is it someone like John Kennedy, Martin Luther King, Billy Graham, or Ronald Reagan? The Bible talks about a great communicator, but it might not be the one you would immediately think of. This person will come at the end of time with a twisted message and a deceptive agenda. He's called the Antichrist.

He will be a world leader and extraordinarily gifted, with charisma and a tremendous intellect. He will appear to be a good man bringing unity to the world, but all the while he is the embodiment of evil. He will prey on the desire for worldwide peace and economic prosperity. But, listen closely to avoid being led astray by someone as evil as the Antichrist. Don't expect him to come with horns and a pitchfork. Judge what he says about Jesus. That will determine if he is truly the Antichrist.

May 5

LIES IN THE DAVINCI CODE

"You shall not bear a false report . . ."
—Exodus 23:1

The *DaVinci Code* is a long-term best seller. Part of the reason for its popularity is that we live in a world where people are fascinated by Jesus, yet they are ignorant of what history and the Bible can teach us. As a result, many lies about Jesus in the *The DaVinci Code* are believed to be true.

The book begins with a lie, stating, "Descriptions of art work, architecture, documents, and secret rituals in this novel are accurate." Dan Brown writes the novel as if it's historical fiction when in reality, it's just fiction. There are speculations about art work, architecture, documents, and secret rituals for which there is either no evidence or these are blatantly false. Then the author proceeds to tell more lies.

It's a hard-to-put-down read, but it adheres to the philosophy of a Nazi Germany propaganda specialist who said, "The bigger the lie, the more it is believed." Sadly, many have believed. But good news! There is a historically accurate book about Jesus and Mary Magdalene. It's called the Bible.

May 6

LIFE CHANGE OF ZACH

*"For the Son of Man has come to seek
and to save that which was lost."*
—Luke 19:10

During Jesus' ministry the crowds around Him were greater than golf fans around Tiger Woods. A short man named Zaccheus was determined to see Him, so he climbed a tree. Not every day does the richest and most despised man in town climb a tree. Jesus saw him and knew he was searching, looking for meaning, something that money and power don't bring. So He asked Zach to lunch. The crowds were appalled, for Zach was such a known sinner. Yet meeting Jesus changed his life—by paying back all those he had defrauded and giving money to the poor. What a change—going from a desire to get, to a desire to give.

Jesus told the crowd He came to seek and save those who were spiritually lost. That's good news for those of you who feel far from God, whom money or power has left feeling empty. Jesus came for people like you. Get to know Him like Zach did and you'll discover the meaning of life.

May 7

THREE KEYS TO A GREAT MARRIAGE

". . . A man shall leave his father and mother
and the two shall become one flesh . . ."
—**Mark 10:7–8**

There is a key verse on marriage that is found only once in the Old Testament and twice in the New. The theme is clear: We are to leave, cleave, and weave.

Leave

A man shall leave his mother and father. This is about prioritizing our spouse over parents, children, siblings, and friends. Our spouse should be our best friend. If you are married, and closer to any person other than your spouse, your priorities are out of whack!

Cleave

Cleave to his wife. The word cleave means to join fast together, to glue, or cement. These definitions imply there will always be pressures to pull the marriage apart. (things like busyness, work, demands from children, money, health problems, infidelity, and so on). In short, marriage is about lifetime commitment.

Weave

The two shall become one flesh. Sexual intimacy and fulfillment is a by-product of a healthy marriage relationship. It symbolizes how a husband and wife become one.

Leave. Cleave. Weave. Three keys to a great marriage.

May 8

GOD KNOWS YOUR NAME

"... the Lord knows those who are His ..."
—2 Timothy 2:19

Years ago the great Methodist preacher Charles Allen was asked by a wealthy Texas oilman who he believed was our greatest president. Dr. Allen said, "That's easy. LBJ."

The man's face turned red with anger. He said, "Dr. Allen, how in the world can you say that lying, scheming scoundrel was our greatest president?"

He replied, "Well, one day I was standing in the lobby of a hotel and LBJ came through. He shouted to me, 'Dr. Allen, you keeping those Methodists straight?' The reason I feel he was the greatest president is because he is the only one who knew my name."

When important people know our name it makes us feel good. But when they call us by name in front of a crowd, we really feel special.

Good news. The most important person who ever lived knows your name. His name is Jesus. He knows everything about you and He loves you anyway. When you get to know him as Savior and Lord, He'll make you feel important and significant, even more than the president, calling you by name.

May 9

FINDING THE RIGHT MATE

"Do not be bound together with unbelievers . . ."
—2 Corinthians 6:14

When it comes to finding the right mate, one of Hollywood's more famous philosophers comes to mind. He says, "Life is like a box of chocolates, you never know what you're going to get."

Amazingly, many approach finding a mate with the Forrest Gump philosophy. But finding the right mate is a biggie! Let me suggest a few thoughts:

- Are you compatible? Do you have similar backgrounds when it comes to faith, education, socio-economics, and interests? Does your giftedness complement your mate?
- Is this person your best friend? If not, you haven't found the right one.
- Do friends and family who know you well affirm the choice?
- Are you excited about spending the rest of your life with this person, no matter what?
- Finally, are you aware of their shortcomings and do you still love them anyway?

If all your answers are "yes," you might have found the right one. If not, you may want to slow down or even call it off. But remember, most of all, seek God's will. He knows you best and knows what is best for you.

May 10

THE BIBLE

"Thy word is a lamp unto my feet, and a light to my path."
—Psalm 119:105

The Bible is the best seller that many people buy but never read. Yet no book is richer or more timeless than the Bible. Listen to what it says:

All Scripture is inspired by God. Amazing! Over forty authors who wrote over a period of 1,600 years were all inspired by the same God to give a clear and coherent message.

It's also profitable for:

- Teaching—about God, man, and life.
- Reproof—it tells us when we go wrong and need to get right.
- Correction—it helps us get on the right track. Like a good doctor, it points out the problem and tells us the cure.
- Training in right living—it's a manual for living in a way that's pleasing to God.

Scripture shows us how we can face every challenge with wisdom and strength. The Bible is a good book. I hope you'll read it with the faith that God wants to speak to you through His Word. You just may find the answer to life.

May 11

THE FATHER'S ROLE IN FAMILY VALUES

"For am I now seeking the favor of men, or of God?"
—Galatians 1:10

The media had a field day in 1999, reporting on a new resolution about the family passed by the Southern Baptists at their convention. The statement that stirred up a hornet's nest was, "A wife is to submit graciously to the servant leadership of her husband."

Think for a moment about the statement in light of the husband and his call to servant leadership in the home. What does this mean? Servant leadership is not the autocratic, dictatorial leadership found in the world. True servant leadership means to lead like Jesus Christ. Men are to love their wives like Christ loves the church. Christ gave His life for the church. What woman would refuse this type of leadership?

Women who are willing to follow Christ are called to submit to their husbands, not because they deserve it (none of us do), but out of submission to Christ.

Men, are you willing to do that for your wife? For your children? Don't focus on what you believe your wife should be doing to submit to you; she will always resent that. Instead, first submit to the Lordship of Christ in your own life. Men, you should seek to submit to Christ. Women, you should seek to submit to Christ. You should both trust His Word to create marital harmony.

Do you have the courage to trust Christ and His Word when it comes to His plan for your marriage? In the twenty-first century, that calls for a radical counter-cultural faith. So who are you going to please? Christ or culture?

May 12

Submission

"Wives, be subject to your own husbands, as to the Lord."
—Ephesians 5:22

One of the most counter-cultural teachings in Scripture is "wives submit to your husbands." Now ladies, before you get bent out of shape, let's remember what the Bible doesn't teach.

It doesn't teach that women are to submit to men. If a Christian man has a female boss, he's called to submit to her authority at work.

It doesn't say men and women are unequal. Men and women are different, but both are made in the image of God; therefore, they are equal before God. The Bible would not prohibit a female president of the United States. There are great women leaders in all walks of life.

But for some reason, God's Word teaches that the husband is to lead in the home. And the way husbands do it best is to submit. Submit to Jesus. The husband is commanded to love his wife like Christ does the church—to be a servant leader, never a dictatorial leader.

But remember—it only works well when both the husband and wife submit to Christ. Are you willing?

May 13

MOTHERHOOD

"Behold children are a gift of the Lord;
the fruit of the womb is a reward."
—**Psalm 127:3**

Dr. Leila Denmark, a well-known Atlanta pediatrician, said, "Every animal on earth takes care of its own until they're able to take care of themselves, except us. We have brainwashed people into thinking that there's something greater out there than being a mother."

Ellen Wilson Fielding, who left her prestigious job as book editor of the *Wall Street Journal* to be at home full-time with her son, came to see it this way: "I felt I was going to a greater thing when I left the *Wall Street Journal* to care for my son." She said, "For the essence of motherhood is the acceptance of God's offer to share in the creation and development of another human being. The question was not whether the job was good enough for me, but whether I was good enough for the job."

Motherhood is the toughest, most demanding, yet most important job in the world. With the many choices for women today, let's not forget that there is no calling of God more important than being a mom.

May 14

Moms Are Important

"Her children rise up and bless her;"
—Proverbs 31:28

When Thomas Edison's intelligent and sympathetic mother learned that his teachers felt he had inferior ability, she educated him at home. He said, "My mother was the making of me. She was so true, so sure of me, that I felt I had someone to live for, someone I must not disappoint." A mother's love and a mother's time are vitally important to the development of a child. Just think of the ways we benefit today from the investment of time on the part of Thomas Edison's mom.

British psychiatrist John Bowlby said, "The young child's hunger for his mother's love and presence is as great as his hunger for food."

Moms, you're pulled in so many different directions today. The stress can be unbelievable, but remember that nothing is more important than the investment of time in the life of your child. God's Word tells us that when a mother does this, her children rise up and call her blessed and her husband praises her, saying, "Many women have done virtuously but you exceed them all."

I'm certainly thankful for my mom and have been tremendously blessed by her love and devotion.

May 15

LEGACY

*"...for he was a faithful man
and feared God more than many."*
—Nehemiah 7:2

As you think of the future, I have a question. What do you plan to leave to your heirs? Stocks and bonds? Property? Investment-quality art? As important as planning for the future is, there is one fact that so many fail to recognize. You're creating a legacy that will live beyond your death. Your character will continue to speak for good or evil after your life on earth has ended.

"Unquestionable character" is one of the greatest gifts we can leave our heirs. So many, by concentrating on amassing financial wealth, fail to help build honesty, responsibility, compassion, or love for God and their fellow man, into the life of their kids.

Character begins with your example—your life. It's more caught than taught, but teaching is important too. You can't leave your heirs a greater gift than this.

Wouldn't you like to know that your life will be remembered for more than money? What a legacy we leave our kids when they reflect on our lives and say, "My mom and dad are the finest people I've ever known."

May 16

WHAT IS HEAVEN LIKE?

"And if I go and prepare a place for you, I will come again, and receive you to Myself; that where I am, there you may be also."
—John 14:3

What is heaven like?

The most common image is a place of clouds where people wear white robes and halos, and do nothing except play harps with goofy smiles on their faces. That's a view of heaven that sounds more like hell to me! What a bore!

What is heaven really like? Jesus spoke very little of it, but He did say this, "In My Father's house are many dwelling places. I go to prepare a place for you." What is heaven like? It's like home, with a loving father. It's a place of security, a permanent place to live, and a place of refuge. There's a longing within all of us to find home. Heaven is like home with a father and loved ones as they're supposed to be.

How can you be sure you'll get to that home? Is there a map or rules to follow? No, it comes through a person, Jesus Christ Himself. As He talked about a heavenly home, He added that He is the only way for us to truly come home.

May 17

A VIEW OF HELL

"... to those who do not obey the gospel of our Lord Jesus. And these will pay the penalty of eternal destruction, away from the presence of the Lord ..."
—2 Thessalonians 1:8–9

Have you ever taken a minute to think about hell—who's going to be there and what is it all about? Did you know that Jesus spoke more about hell than He did about heaven?

Jesus tells an interesting parable about a rich man and a beggar named Lazarus. The beggar sat each day at the gate of the rich man's house, hoping for some leftovers from the rich man's feast, but they never came. Both men died. Lazarus, the poor man, went to be with God, and the rich man went to hell. Seeing Lazarus across a great divide, he begged that Lazarus might dip his finger in water and bring even a drop to cool his tongue because of the agony of the heat, but it was too late. They were separated by the great divide—forever.

Many people act like hell doesn't exist. They believe everyone eventually goes to heaven because God is love. What if they're wrong? Jesus believed in hell. Do you believe He was wrong or do you believe He tells the truth?

A truth about eternity: until you believe in the bad news of hell, you can't understand the good news of Jesus. He came to save us from hell and guarantee us a place in heaven. The question is: what do you believe about hell? What Jesus says or something else?

May 18

WORK—A CALLING OR A CURSE?

*"Whatever you do, do your work heartily,
as for the Lord rather than for men;"*
—Colossians 3:23

Do you see work as a calling or a curse? Is your only reason for working to make a living, or do you live for your work? Is your work drudgery or fulfilling, monotonous or challenging? One thing is certain, it was never meant by God to be a curse. He invented it.

When man was placed in the Garden at the beginning of time, God told him to care for it and cultivate it. Obviously, that called for work. After man sinned, God said work would be harder, but He still meant it for good.

So how can we have a healthy view of work?

Listen to the words of Scripture: "Whatever you do, work at it with all your heart, as working for the Lord, not for men." When we adopt that view, no matter how difficult, monotonous, or challenging the work, our motivation changes. To work heartily to please God is the key to finding meaning in work.

Whatever you are, be it a plumber or a president, a carpenter or a teacher, a janitor or CEO, see your work as a calling and a privilege to serve God by doing your best.

May 19

STOCK MARKET

"He who loves money will not be satisfied with money,
nor he who loves abundance with its income."
—Ecclesiastes 5:10

Are you bullish or bearish? Is the Federal Reserve on the right track or not? When you think about the Dow Jones, is it buy or sell? Hold or liquidate? As important as financial advice from Wall Street is, there's a more reliable place to gain understanding on managing our money. That place is the Bible. Amazingly, Jesus speaks more about money and possessions than He does about heaven or hell.

The problem is, we don't want to do it God's way. God's way says to give and share and provide for those who have less. It's advice diametrically opposed to what human reason tells us—to get, to keep, to hoard. God's way is to spend less than we earn. The world's way is to build up that debt. Charge it, baby!

Face it. The best financial planner is the Creator of the world. Why not learn what He has to say about managing money and then try it His way? It's always best.

May 20

Honoring Our Soldiers

"Be devoted to one another in brotherly love;
give preference to one another in honor;"
—Romans 12:10

It's always appropriate to take a moment to remember those who have put their lives on the line to preserve our freedom and to give thanks for those who have given their lives for their country.

We should especially honor those who served in Vietnam. Never has our nation acted so shamefully as it did to the men and women in uniform who served in that conflict. They served in a war they did not start, to preserve freedom for those they did not know; yet time and again our soldiers returned home, only to be spat upon by citizens of this land.

Chances are, you know someone who served in Vietnam and never considered the trauma they faced, not only in war, but caught in the crossfire of a nation divided when they returned home. Always honor those who have given their lives for their nation. But let us especially take time to thank those who put their lives on the line in Vietnam.

If you were one who served, I salute you. If you know someone who did, it's time to say thanks.

May 21

SABBATH

". . . He rested on the seventh day from all His work which He had done."
—Genesis 2:2

In the 1920's, George Bernard Shaw predicted that in the 1980's the workday would last no more than two hours. He thought advanced technology would bring this about. Shaw was a bright man, but a poor futurist. People are working longer hours in spite of all the technological inventions to save us time. As a result, leisure gets squeezed out.

God's Word is clear about the need for balance between work and leisure. Hard work is good, but God's gift to us, to bring balance to our lives, is the Sabbath. Everyone needs at least one day a week to rest from his or her regular job. To enjoy this gift requires discipline. To ignore it is to hit the wall of burnout. Here's the really good news—if you maintain this weekly discipline you'll be better at work.

Do you have that balance between work and rest? Ask God to help you enjoy a weekly day of rest—a Sabbath. You'll be glad you did.

May 22

DISCOURAGEMENT

". . . hope does not disappoint, because the love of God
has been poured out within our hearts . . ."
—Romans 5:5

Do you ever feel discouraged?
We all do. When you feel discouraged, start by looking outside.
Look up. Oak trees abound, and they cause us to look up.

That oak tree is pointing to heaven. Focus on God, our Creator. He promises that "we can do all things in His strength."

Practice prayer as the first resort, not the last. God is interested in anything that interests you. Talk to Him about your concerns. Ask Him to fill you with His Holy Spirit, the Encourager and Comforter.

Get enough rest. Fatigue makes cowards of us all. When our bodies and minds are rested, we view circumstances differently.

Refuse to quit. Keep on keeping on! Perseverance produces character, and character, hope. Hope comes in trusting God to see us through. And remember: an oak tree is just a little nut that refused to give up!

If you're dealing with discouragement, look to God. He'll give you the strength to knock discouragement on its face.

May 23

Parenting Parents

*"And just as you want people to treat you,
treat them in the same way."*
—Luke 6:31

There are few greater challenges in the parent-child relationship than parenting our parents. It involves a role reversal that neither the parent nor the child wants. Yet it's part of honoring our parents. It is caring for them when they are unable to care for themselves.

But difficult questions arise. When does the adult child intervene? Should the parent live with the adult child, or just nearby? There are no easy answers but I offer some suggestions to the question, "How can I best honor my parents by caring for their needs?"

- We honor our parents when we put their needs over what they or we want.
- Our parents need the gift of our time, love, and sacrifice—something they did for us when we were children.
- How we care for our aging parents is how our children learn to honor us when we're no longer able to care for ourselves.

Parenting our parents has long-term implications for our families, our nation, and us.

May 24

INFERTILITY

"Cast your burden upon the LORD and He will sustain you;
He will never allow the righteous to be shaken."
—Psalm 55:22

Infertility is a very common problem with couples wanting to have children. It was also a very common problem among great women of the Bible like Sarah, Rebekah, Rachel, Hannah, and Elizabeth. In biblical days, it was seen as a lack of favor from God. Thankfully, that is not the case today. But the frustration of those unable to have children is very much the same.

If you are struggling with this problem:

1. Study the great women of faith in God's Word and see what God reveals to you.
2. Ask God to create life where there is barrenness.
3. Seek God's guidance on waiting on Him, seeking fertility treatment, or adopting a child in need of parents.
4. Most of all, trust God to know what is best for your life—even if it is not what you want. For this is real faith.

May 25

LIVING TOGETHER

"Commit your way to the Lord, trust also in Him,
and He will do it."
—Psalm 37:5

In June of 2001, *USA Today* revealed the disturbing results of a poll about how twenty-somethings in America feel about living together. Sixty-two percent said living together before marriage is a good way to avoid divorce. And forty-three percent (almost half) said they would *only* marry someone if that person agreed to live together first. These are troubling statistics that show a deep-seated fear of commitment and trust in marriage. But it is an understandable result of so many who were scarred by their own parents' divorce or troubled home.

Couples living together want sex, companionship, and love. They'll get sex and companionship, but they'll never experience real love without commitment. For without commitment, there is no real love. Living together, by definition, is always looking for a way out. No commitment. No trust. No real love.

God's way is love and commitment *first*, and then companionship and sex. And that sex will be far better because of the trust in Him and in your spouse.

Laziness Vs. Workaholism— Finding the Right Balance

*"Six days you shall labor and do all your work,
but the seventh day is a sabbath of the Lord your God;"*
—Exodus 20:9,10

All of us want to be successful when it comes to our work, but let's think about the two most common problems when it comes to work.

One is laziness. We live in a society that so often glorifies the irresponsible—those who won't work—as victims. This is insulting to those who are truly unable to work. God's Word is clear; laziness is not good. God wants us to work hard.

At the other extreme is workaholism, and there are four common traits of the workaholic:

1. Tends to be the first person at the office and the last to leave.
2. Tries to please others, and has a tough time saying no.
3. Tends to only talk about work.
4. Feels guilty taking a day off.

Neither workaholism or laziness is God's intention. The right balance is working hard to please God yet taking time to back away and rest. Take a weekly Sabbath. It is one of God's great ideas for successful living. When we do, we find ourselves refreshed and ready to give our best to our work.

May 27

ALL THINGS WORK FOR GOOD?

"And we know that God causes all things to work together
for good to those who love God,
to those who are called according to His purpose."
—Romans 8:28

Some people believe the Bible teaches, "All things work together for good," but this is nuts! All things don't work together for good for those who die and wind up in hell!

What the Bible does teach is that all things can work together for good for those who love God and are living in His will. We have to love God through Jesus Christ and live according to His teaching in Scripture. To believe anything or to live any way we want nullifies the truth of this verse.

But when we love God and are living for Him, then with any tragedy, any suffering, God can bring good. For with every tragedy and every setback, our choice is to grow bitter or to trust God to bring good out of the greatest grief and difficulty. I hope you'll choose to trust God, even when life doesn't make sense. Look for the good that God can bring.

May 28

GETTING THROUGH GRIEF

"Blessed are those who mourn, for they shall be comforted."
—Matthew 5:4

Losing a loved one or close friend is never easy. If you have recently faced the death of someone you love, or know someone who has, understanding the stages of grief can help.

Grief involves:

- Numbness—an inability to feel when the news of death arrives.
- Denial—a sense of disbelief that the person is really gone.
- Tearful emotion—the reality of permanent separation sets in.
- Anger—a hurt at God or at life as the world continues and you are hurting so badly.
- Depression—a feeling there is little reason to live. Life may seem meaningless when the loss of a loved one has occurred.
- Acceptance—coming to terms with the loss and beginning to move on.

The grieving process takes time, sometimes months and sometimes years, but it can be overcome. The greatest strength for getting through it can be found in the Lord. Remember, God understands grief. He knows what it's like to have a child die. He saw His own Son, Jesus, die for us all. He loves you and wants to help you overcome your grief. Just tell Him you need His help.

MEMORIAL DAY

"Greater love has no one than this,
that one lay down his life for his friends."
—John 15:13

As we come to another Memorial Day, it's appropriate to take a moment to say a word of thanks to those who have put their lives on the line to preserve our freedom. Give thanks for those who have given their lives for their country. We think about those who did this in World Wars I and II, in Korea, in Vietnam, in the Gulf War and most recently in Iraq.

We remember those who gave their lives in these wars. Jesus said, "Greater love has no man than this, that one lay down his life for his friends." Certainly these have set the example in service to our nation. But Jesus Christ has set the ultimate example in giving His life for all mankind.

On Memorial Day, we honor those who gave their lives for our nation. As we remember them, think about the One who gave His life for our salvation.

May 30

Help Me with My Prayer Life

"Pray, then, in this way . . ."
—**Matthew 6:9**

People often ask me questions about prayer. Jesus' disciples asked Him how to pray, for they saw that He often got away to pray. Here is a summary of what Jesus said to do:

Address God as Father. Through Jesus, we can know God personally as our Father—the embodiment of the ideal dad.

Praise. Praise His name and character traits. It makes our problems seem small when we remember how great God is.

Pray for His will to be done. This begins with us but carries over to praying for others.

Pray for daily needs. God wants to meet our needs, but don't confuse needs and wants.

Confess your sins. Ask God's forgiveness and ask God's help in forgiving others who wrong you.

Ask for protection and strength in the face of temptation and evil.

Jesus teaches the basics on prayer. Find a quiet spot and give it a try. And, remember, a prayer life gets better with practice.

GARTH AND UNANSWERED PRAYER

"Call to Me, and I will answer you,
and I will tell you great and mighty things,
which you do not know."
—Jeremiah 33:3

In Garth Brooks' hit "Unanswered Prayer," he sings of how thankful he is that God didn't answer his prayer to marry his high school honey. Instead, God led him to meet and marry the right woman for him. The song has good insight about God. He only wants what is best for us.

God answers prayer. Every single time. He does it in three main ways: yes, no, and wait awhile.

If it's *yes,* do we have the courage to move ahead in faith?

If *no,* are we willing to trust that God knows best, and accept it?

It may not be what we want, but it will always be for our best. This is what Garth calls "unanswered prayer." And if the answer is *wait awhile,* are we willing to do that?

June 1

GOD HEARS ALL

". . . do not swear, either by heaven or by earth or with any other oath; but let your yes be yes, and your no, no . . ."
—James 5:12

One of the common responses I often hear from someone I've just met and am about to play a tennis match or a golf game against says, "Oh, I've got to watch my language today." Or in the course of the match, curse words will fly and he'll say, "Pastor, I'm so sorry."

My response is usually, "Don't worry about me. God is the one you need to be concerned about. He hears everything."

Usually the person will look at me with big eyes like, "I hadn't thought about that." And bless his heart, he sometimes becomes so unsettled trying to take all that in, that he gets off his game a bit.

God hears all, knows all, sees all, and is over all. Everything we've done or said is recorded in His book of our life. Yet He loves us anyway. He loves us so much that He sent His Son to pay the penalty for our sins so we can be forgiven. That includes every bad thing we've said or done. Our choice is whether to accept His love and grace in faith!

Best Friends in Marriage

"I thank my God in all my remembrance of you . . ."
—Philippians 1:3

The Bible repeatedly says of marriage that "a man shall leave his father and mother and cleave to his wife." The message is clear; our *spouse* should be our best friend. If they are not, we need to get this right.

What are some qualities of a best friend?

- *A desire to be together.* A weekly date is key to staying in love with your mate.
- *Great communication.* Best friends can talk about anything.
- *Loyalty.* Best friends are loyal. They keep confidences.
- *Willingness to forgive.* They accept one another and are so committed to the friendship, they choose to forgive and work through it, even when the other friend lets them down.

Is your spouse your best friend? If so, thank God for a marriage like He has in mind. If not, ask God to forgive you and to help you forgive your spouse, and make a commitment with your spouse to become best friends.

June 3

END OF THE WORLD

*"The Lord is not slow about His promise,
as some count slowness, but is patient toward you,
not wishing for any to perish but for all to come to repentance."*
—2 Peter 3:9

There's a lot of focus these days on doomsday scenarios. Movies like *Armageddon* and *Deep Impact* envision a giant meteor headed right for the earth to destroy the world. Others worry that nuclear weapons will fall into the hands of terrorists, and boom! It's all over.

What do you think?

God destroyed the world once with a flood when mankind was so bad they made Him sick. In the end, God will destroy the world with fire. But there's a reason He hasn't done it yet. Consider His words: "He is waiting because He desires for none to perish and He is giving more time for sinners to repent." That's in the Bible.

Hey, is that you? God loves each of you so much He wants all to be saved by Him, but His patience will eventually wear out because of the evil of our world. When it does, will you be toast or will you be safe in heaven?

June 4

HOW GOD MEASURES A MAN

". . . for God sees not as man sees,
for man looks at the outward appearance,
but the Lord looks at the heart.'"
—1 Samuel 16:7

How do you measure the worth of another person? Is it by their wealth, their position, their fame, their looks, their education, or their success?

I don't know how you would answer that question, but I can tell you how God measures the worth of a person. God's Word says, "God does not see man as man sees him. For man looks at the outward appearance, but the Lord looks at the heart."

The heart speaks of a person's character, courage and spirit. So often when we measure the worth of a person we just look at the outward appearance, but God looks at the inside.

If that's the case, how does He measure you? If you had a heart exam today, what kind of heart would God find? The good news is this: God has given us a way to have a new heart and it's found through faith in Jesus Christ.

It's an interesting insight into life that when we begin to have the right heart through Christ, we begin to measure the worth of others God's way.

June 5

ADULTERY PREVENTION

"Submit therefore to God.
Resist the devil and he will flee from you."
—James 4:7

It's obvious that in America today, marriage is no longer held in honor. Divorce became acceptable long ago. Now America is accepting yet another taboo—adultery. Though adultery doesn't seem to matter to many, it still matters to God. His Word says, "Let marriage be held in honor among all."

In that light, let me suggest a few thoughts on preventing adultery:

- Adultery doesn't begin with sexual intercourse. It begins when you make an emotional connection with a person who is not your spouse. Ask yourself, "Would I want my spouse to see me interacting with this person this way?"
- Seek to stay out of vulnerable situations where the temptation to be unfaithful increases.
- Stay in close communication with your spouse. Adultery always involves lies.
- Remember that true love equals commitment to your spouse.
- Seek to please God most of all.

When we seek to please God first, we just don't have to worry about adultery. But when we seek to please self, we always do.

June 6

SIMPLE THINGS

"... Here am I. Send me!"
—Isaiah 6:8

Do you think that someday you will be able to do something great for God? Maybe you will write a huge check to your favorite charity or possibly fund a program to feed the hungry. Perhaps you might help a special ministry at your church.

Many people waste so much time waiting until they *can* do something big that they miss opportunities for service right now. This attitude is the opposite of the one that the Bible teaches. Jesus took simple things from ordinary folks and turned them into resources beyond imagination.

One day a little boy overheard the disciples of Jesus trying to figure out how they were going to feed 5,000 families. The boy offered his lunch of five loaves and two fish to help. When Jesus received it, He multiplied it into enough food to feed 5,000 families—with leftovers.

This same Jesus can turn the simple things you bring to Him, those deeds of service day by day, and multiply them into great blessings for you, as well as for others. As small as it may seem, He is looking for people who will give Him all they have, and trust Him to do the rest.

June 7

PEACE

"Peace I leave with you;
My peace I give you; not as the world gives . . ."
—John 14:27

When Israel and the PLO signed the peace treaty on the White House lawn, it was an amazing moment. Time will tell if a peace treaty works, for peace in our world is elusive and difficult to grasp.

Remember, peace is not the absence of conflict—that's called a truce. Peace is reconciliation between two estranged parties. Reconciliation means to become one or to become friends, which is very different from a truce.

In that light, I propose to you that man will never find lasting peace until he finds peace within himself, and we can't find peace within until we find peace with God. That peace is found through the person of Jesus Christ.

Christ did not come to bring peace on earth through peace treaties, but He came to reconcile sinful individuals with God. With that comes true inner peace. With inner peace comes the ability to live in peace with our fellow man.

June 8

BEING BORN IN THE FAMILY THAT LASTS

"Jesus called for them saying, 'Permit the children to come to Me, and do not hinder them.'"
—Luke 18:16

Few things in life inspire a couple more than giving birth to a child. It's one of those times when even a skeptic tends to believe in God. But as awesome as it is to be blessed with children, it's doubly awesome to know that your child has been born into the family of God.

This hit home on a trip to Israel when my three sons were baptized in the Jordan River as a testimony of their faith in Jesus Christ. My heart was overflowing, knowing that all of them, at different points in their lives, had been born into the family of God through faith in Christ. My wife and I have not only had the blessing of these sons being born into our family, but of knowing that they're in the family of God forever.

Have your children been born into the family of God? Have you? It comes through faith in Christ. Childbirth is great, but being born into the family that lasts forever is the greatest.

June 9

FRIENDSHIP

> *"But there is a friend who sticks closer than a brother."*
> **—Proverbs 18:24**

A real friend is one of life's greatest blessings. In this day of temporary relationships, true friendship is rare. How can you find and develop lasting friendships? Proverbs gives us some guidance:

To have a friend, be a friend. Go out of your way to show that you are interested in their lives. Ask questions.

To cement a friendship, be loyal. Demonstrate your willingness to love them unconditionally, even when your friend is not lovable. Be supportive even when your friend is not popular.

To experience lasting friendship, be an encourager. A true friend is someone who tells the truth, but always with your best interests at heart.

There is someone who wants to be your friend, who is interested in you, who is loyal and supportive, and encourages you to do your best. That person is Jesus Christ. Decide today to let Him be your best friend.

June 10

LEAVE, CLEAVE, AND ONE

"For this cause a man shall leave his father and his mother, and shall cleave to his wife; and they shall become one flesh."
—Genesis 2:24

One verse on marriage appears in the Bible three times. It must be important. It goes like this: "For this cause a man shall leave his father and mother and shall cleave to his wife; and the two shall become one flesh." Let's look at that.

Leave. When you get married, there needs to be an emotional withdrawal from parents and other meaningful relationships as you prioritize your spouse. Your spouse needs to be your closest friend.

Cleave. Marriage is a total commitment—a lifetime commitment. Without this commitment, divorce will often result.

One flesh. Sexual fulfillment is the result of a couple being best friends and totally committed to each other in a marital relationship. Otherwise, sex is second best. Sex is God's idea, so trust Him on this.

Leave, plus cleave, equals one. This is God's simple plan for a meaningful marriage.

June 11

FATHERS AND CHILDREN

"Fathers, do not exasperate your children,
that they may not lose heart."
—Colossians 3:21

Dads, looking for a little help in being a good father? One particular verse from the Bible really helps: "Fathers, don't provoke your children, instead bring them up in the discipline and instruction of the Lord."

1. *Don't provoke your children.* That means don't make unrealistic demands. Don't crush their spirit by being aloof or overly strict. Every child has a fragile psyche that needs to be built up, not torn down.
2. *Bring them up in discipline.* Discipline should be fair and consistent. They need to know the boundaries and know there are negative consequences if they ignore them. This gives children security and helps them know they are loved.
3. *. . . and the instruction of the Lord.* Discipline precedes instruction—any good teacher knows that. But discipline without instruction exasperates children. They need Dad to teach them right from wrong, and to do it with love.

It's not easy being a good dad but we sure have a great model in our heavenly Father revealed to us through Jesus.

June 12

THE PERFECT BODY

"... for the trumpet will sound, and the dead will be raised imperishable, and we shall be changed."
—1 Corinthians 15:52

In our culture today, we get hit with a lot of information about how to have the perfect body. If you watch cable TV, you'll see that for a mere $19.95 and fifteen minutes a day, some fitness machine will give you the perfect body. But I have bad news for you. Even though some of you may come closer to the perfect body than others, no one in this life will ever permanently achieve it. For all of us, our bodies will eventually wear out.

One day when Jesus returns, the Christian will be given the perfect body. Jesus Christ promised we will receive a new body that never wears out. It comes with a new mind that never struggles with envy, hatred, or any of life's sins. A perfect ten of a body that never tires, that never wears out—I could sure use that!

We are to take care of our bodies today, even though they will wear out. But don't miss the big picture! Live with the hope of Jesus' promise that one day those who know Him in a personal way will receive the perfect body. A body that lasts!

June 13

AFTERSHOCKS OF DIVORCE

*"For if you forgive men for their transgressions,
your heavenly Father will also forgive you."*
—Matthew 6:14

Those who have experienced an earthquake know it can be shocking. Yet sometimes it's the aftershocks that send people over the edge. Divorce is similar. The initial break is traumatic but the aftershocks can be devastating. The emotional trauma brings on grief, numbness, anger, guilt, and depression, as well as long-term negative effects on children, financial destruction, and loneliness. These aftershocks are just some of the reasons why God hates divorce. But remember, God doesn't hate the divorced person. God will help you overcome the aftershocks if you remember to seek His forgiveness—ask for His help to forgive yourself as well as to forgive your ex.

If you're a child of divorce, remember it's not your fault. Choose to seek God's help with forgiving your parents, and always seek the help of others when you need it. Remember, God loves you and wants you to overcome the aftershocks of divorce. Since He overcame a cross with the empty tomb, He can certainly give you victory in this area.

June 14

Taking Care of Our Bodies

". . . your body is a temple of the Holy Spirit . . ."
—1 Corinthians 6:19

In the seventies and early eighties, a new craze began to sweep the nation. It was called the fitness craze. The number of joggers went from thousands of oddballs to millions dashing across the landscape of America. That was a good thing, for taking care of our bodies is an important spiritual principle.

Think about the most common ways people abuse their bodies—smoking, alcohol and drug abuse, lack of regular exercise, and of course, over and undereating. One thing about overeating and undereating is it is evident to all. Certainly, preachers who rail against the evils of alcohol while standing there so fat and out of shape that they make a hog look petite are a living display of hypocrisy; gluttony is just as real a sin as drunkenness. Today I urge you to make a decision. Get in shape. Take care of your body. It's an important spiritual discipline.

June 15

WHAT IS GOOD?

*"And what does the Lord require of you but to do justice,
to love kindness, and to walk humbly with your God?"*
—**Micah 6:8**

What is your definition of being good? What would you say if asked? Years ago, a great Jewish prophet gave the answer. He said, "God has shown you what is good, to act justly, love mercy, and walk humbly with your God." Let's look at those more specifically.

To act justly. We need to be honest and fair with every person, and seek to bring justice for those who are mistreated or taken advantage of.

To love mercy: We all mess up, and when we do we sure appreciate someone who is compassionate and forgiving. Forgiveness doesn't mean consequences are removed. Forgiveness, though, doesn't seek revenge. Compassion is an attitude of the heart.

Walk humbly with your God: When a person has no fear of God, that person makes himself God and will rationalize all kinds of evil. But to live in a way to please God, seen perfectly in Jesus, is a good way to live.

To act justly, to love mercy, and to walk humbly with God, that's God's answer to what is good.

June 16

WHO KNOWS YOU?

"Before I formed you in the womb I knew you.
And before you were born I consecrated you;
I have appointed you a prophet to the nations."
—Jeremiah 1:5

Who really knows you and the thoughts of your heart and the secret things you intentionally keep hidden from others? Do you share your innermost thoughts with anyone?

Some may say it's their spouse or a best friend. Yet, I suggest that even though you may think you know yourself well and that others see the real you, no one knows you more completely than the One who created you.

God says, "Before I formed you in the womb I knew you." It only makes sense that to know and understand ourselves, we need a personal relationship with the One who knows us best.

The good news is that God knows us best, and loves us more than anyone else. He knows our failings and our shortcomings and loves us anyway. Through Jesus Christ, we have the privilege of having a personal relationship with our Creator. That relationship begins when we accept God's love through faith. It's a relationship that lasts forever and that's mighty good news.

June 17

MAXIMUM SEX

"... the Lord has been a witness between you and the wife of
your youth ... she is your companion
and your wife by covenant."
—Malachi 2:14

Hey, let's talk maximum sex.

In a day of so much sexual misunderstanding, we need to look to the One who invented it. In this area, Hollywood constantly perpetuates myths and misunderstandings.

Psychology Today reported in a survey that ninety-four percent of television soap operas are about love between partners who are not married to each other. This is just the opposite of what the Inventor of sex had in mind. When God created mankind, He said, "... a man shall leave his father and mother and be united to his wife, and they will become one flesh."

- Sex is a gift of God to be enjoyed in the context of committed love in marriage.
- Maximum sex is a by-product of a meaningful relationship with one's spouse. You are best friends, physically attracted to one another, and committed for life.
- God's Word goes on to warn that sex outside the context of marriage is filled with problems.

For maximum sex, trust the Inventor of sex! He knows what's best!

June 18

DISCOVERING YOUR LIFE'S PURPOSE

"For I know the plans I have for you," declares the Lord,
"plans for welfare and not for calamity
to give you a future and a hope."
—Jeremiah 29:11

Why were you born? What is your life's purpose? Can you write it down in a phrase or a sentence? Let's fast forward. What do you want on your tombstone? What few words would describe your priorities or your passion?

Clarity of purpose is a key to successful living:

- It guides us in our decision-making.
- It helps us to know when to say yes and when to say no.
- It determines where we will go in life. It's the difference between just existing and making a difference.
- Only through our Creator can we find our ultimate purpose; He created us for a purpose. No one is here by accident. God has a plan for every life—a destiny to fulfill.

What's yours?

I can't answer that question for you, but the One who created you can. Get to know Him through His Son Jesus, and His ever-insightful word in Scripture. You'll be taking the first and most important step in discovering your life's purpose.

June 19

The Road to Financial Security

"How blessed is the man who finds wisdom,
and the man who gains understanding."
—Proverbs 3:13

Are you on the road to financial security? Let me suggest a few goals to strive for in seeking personal financial security.

- You need to know what you make, and if you're on commission, estimate conservatively what it'll be.
- Spend less than you earn. I know it seems obvious, but it is so overlooked that it has to be mentioned.
- Have a personal or family budget. Budgets help us prioritize and meet our goals.
- In developing that budget, focus on four major categories:

  - a goal for giving
  - an estimated amount for taxes
  - a goal for savings and investments
  - fixed expenses, such as car, house, groceries, etc.

What's left is discretionary income and you will want to set goals in this area. It includes such items as clothing, furniture, vacation, and entertainment.

From where does all this practical insight come? It's based on principles right out of the Bible. You'll be amazed that when you look to Scripture, you'll find the keys to financial security.

June 20

HOW TO BE LIKE THE DEVIL

"Whoever secretly slanders his neighbor,
him [the Lord] will destroy; no one who has a haughty look
and an arrogant heart will [the Lord] endure."
—Psalm 101:5

Do you want to live like the devil? For some of us, that's easy. For all of us, we come by it naturally. But there are two character traits that make us most like Satan:

1. Pride: C. S. Lewis said, "The utmost evil is pride. Unchastity, anger, greed, drunkenness . . . are mere flea bites in comparison. It was through pride that the devil became the devil. It is the complete anti-God state of mind." Pride is thinking more highly of ourselves than we should—feeling we are better than others. It is arrogant conceit. Pride is, most of all, feeling no need for God, considering yourself self-reliant. The person filled with this kind of pride is most like the Devil himself.
2. Malicious gossip or slander: The Greek word for this is diabolos, also translated "the Devil." People who gossip and slander others are like the Devil. In short, he's just a big liar.

Pride, malicious gossip, and lying are character traits that make us most like the Devil. Man made in the image of God looks pretty good, but when man resembles the Devil he sure is ugly. Who do you look like?

W.W.J.D.

"... do not imitate what is evil, but what is good."
—3 John 1:11

Have you thought about the current epidemic we face as parents in this generation? There is more violence, sex, and immorality bombarding a child's intellect than ever. Look at the results: We see children committing vicious murders, including killing their classmates, with little regard for their actions. Obviously, they are conditioned by what they see on TV and in the movies.

Do you remember George Orwell's book, *1984?* When it came out in 1949, the world was shocked because he predicted that people would go to the movies and laugh at people being killed. That prediction has become reality. It's called "the numbing of America."

There is a remedy. As a parent, you can teach your children to make decisions based on a formula—WWJD—What Would Jesus Do? Can you think of any wrong your child might learn by doing this?

WWJD? The Bible shows us. Teach it to your child as a formula for learning right from wrong.

What's in a Name?

"A good name is to be more desired than great riches . . ."
—Proverbs 22:1

What's in a name? A person's name carries a lot of meaning. What does your name bring to mind?

In the Bible, Solomon said, "A good name is better than a good ointment." In the ancient world, they would often use very rare oils and sweet-smelling perfumes on special occasions—not every day, like we use perfume or after-shave today. Solomon wants us to understand that, even as precious and expensive as those items were, their value didn't compare to a good name.

You can put on perfume and you'll smell good for a short time, but a good name is lasting. It stays with you wherever you go, in every setting in life.

What do people think when they hear your name? Is it good or bad? I have good news. When you put God first and follow His teaching, over time He'll help you develop a good name.

June 23

MORE OBJECTIONS TO CHRISTIANITY

"... that which is known about God is evident within them; for God made it evident to them."
—Romans 1:19

One objection to Christianity is that Christ is the only way to God. That raises another question: If Christ is the only way, what about all the people who live in remote areas of the world who never have heard of Jesus? Will they be damned to hell?

That's a good question. I do know this: the Bible teaches us that we have a loving and just God. Is a just God going to condemn people who never had an opportunity to hear of Christ? They certainly can't help that. But in the book of Romans, chapter one, Scripture does say every person will be accountable to God with the knowledge they have. Let's just trust God to be fair.

Remember, you *have* heard of Jesus, and because of that, you're responsible to choose whether you're going to follow Christ or not. When you do choose to follow Christ, you can join with other Christians in getting the Good News out to those who have never heard. It's Good News all need to hear—that Christ is the way to know God.

June 24

HUMILITY

"The reward of humility and the fear of the Lord are riches, honor and life."
—**Proverbs 22:4**

Humility. It's the one trait that when we think we've got it, we've lost it. But humility is not a false sense of modesty. This puts off other people and insults God, our Creator, for He has given us all gifts and abilities.

So what is humility? It's a realistic view of ourselves—knowing our strengths and weaknesses. It's being modest about our strengths and honest about our weaknesses. It's doing our best, but not taking ourselves too seriously.

Atlanta's Bobby Jones was perhaps the greatest golfer of all time. He faced a long-term debilitating illness in the final years of his life. Herbert Warren Wind said of him, "As a young man, he was able to stand up to just about the best that life could offer, which isn't easy, and later stood up with equal grace to just about the worst." That's humility. Greatness with humility is greatness indeed.

June 25

HYPOCRITICAL PREACHERS AND RELIGIOUS LEADERS

"If someone says, 'I love God' and hates his brother,
he is a liar . . ."
—1 John 4:20

Don't you just hate hypocrisy in the church? For many of you it's a major reason why you don't go to church. In the movie *The Apostle,* starring Robert Duvall, we see a preacher who gets in trouble. He even kills a man, but he runs to a new town and continues to preach.

Certainly, over the last thirty years, Hollywood has done a number on preachers and priests. And time after time they are painted in a very unflattering way, usually as hypocrites or a bunch of out-of-touch airheads, or mean, cruel sickos. If you combine all of that with the charlatan TV evangelists, it's not a pretty picture.

The truth is, all of us preachers struggle with hypocrisy, not always practicing what we preach. I sure do. But I have good news. I've only known one preacher in my life who had no trace of hypocrisy. And He's alive today—His name is Jesus. All the rest of us fall short, but Jesus never does. So put your focus and your faith in Him.

June 26

REVENGE—
THE WRONG WAY TO PRAY

"Do not judge lest you will be judged.
For in the same way you judge, you will be judged;
and by your standard of measure, it will be measured to you."
—Matthew 7:1–2

Do you ever wish that certain people got what you felt they deserved—especially people who have wronged you? Do some people seem to get away with murder and not face any kind of punishment or repercussion?

You may have seen the cartoon with three panels:

Panel 1: A zealous character is praying to the Almighty. He says, "God, smite my worst enemy!"
Panel 2: The man praying this prayer is struck by lightning.
Panel 3: The man groggily says, "God, let me rephrase that!"

Be careful what you pray for because sometimes you might find your own worst enemy is yourself. Jesus Christ says, "Do not judge lest you be judged. For in the way you judge others you will be judged as well."

I hope that today you won't be so hard on others, because one day the gavel may fall on you.

June 27

Sibling Rivalry

"Am I my brother's keeper?"
—Genesis 4:9

Do you ever struggle with sibling rivalry with your own siblings or with your kids? This can be especially tough with siblings of the same sex who are close in age. The Bible is filled with great stories of sibling rivalries: Cain and Abel, Jacob and Esau, Joseph and his brothers, David and his brothers. What can we learn?

- Sibling rivalries happen in the best of families.
- Perhaps they most commonly result from competition and jealousy.
- Parents can exasperate it by showing favoritism, comparing one child to another, or trying to manipulate God's will for one child over another.

Sibling rivalry can be overcome when parents are fair and teach siblings to respect and love one another. They can teach siblings to forgive and seek forgiveness of one another. When that occurs, it's like seeing the face of God.

June 28

FAITH IN ACTION

> *"... when the soles of the feet ... shall rest in the waters of*
> *the Jordan, the waters of the Jordan shall be cut off,*
> *and the waters which are flowing down from above*
> *shall stand in one heap."*
> —Joshua 3:13

Faith requires action. After forty years, the children of Israel had been led out of the wilderness and now found themselves on the banks of a swollen Jordan River. The Promised Land was just on the other side. Oh so close, yet so far away! A huge obstacle separated them from the blessing God had promised. Standing on the bank of the raging river, wringing their hands and praying would not solve their problem. They had to act. And it was not until, in faith, they stepped into the turbulent waters that the river stood on end and the people walked into the Promised Land on dry land.

So it is with our lives. Obstacles separate us from God's richest blessings. To simply have faith that God will provide a way doesn't always make a way. To stand by until God makes a way obvious may cause us to delay His blessing. It takes both faith and action to experience God's best.

Don't fall victim to the paralysis of analysis. Go for it as God leads!

June 29

Abolishing Death

". . . there shall no longer be any death . . .
the first things have passed away."
—Revelation 21:4

The second coming of Jesus Christ is one of the central themes of Christianity and will be the culmination of history as we know it. Christ will establish His kingdom on earth, overcome the Antichrist and the forces of evil, and bring justice and peace. The great enemy of God and man will be abolished. As is written in the Word of God, "Then comes the end . . . He must reign until He has put all enemies under His feet. The last enemy that will be abolished is death."

What a great day it will be for all of Jesus' followers! Death will be abolished. There will be no more tears, no more grief, and no more separation from loved ones. When you say the Lord's Prayer, "Thy kingdom come, Thy will be done on earth as it is in heaven," you're praying for Jesus to come again and establish His kingdom. To experience God's will on earth as it is in heaven means no more death. Jesus is the first to conquer death. His followers will do the same.

June 30

THE ULTIMATE FAMILY REUNION

"I say to you, that many shall come from east and west,
and recline at the table with Abraham, and Isaac,
and Jacob in the kingdom of heaven."
—Matthew 8:11

Family reunions can be fun or miserable. Whether they're good or bad depends on you, members of your family, or both. But I want to tell you about the ultimate family reunion.

I'm speaking of what happens when Christians die. Not only do we get to be with Christ, we also get to be with those who have died in Christ before us and are enjoying the eternal family reunion in heaven—a reunion where everyone gets along. Won't that be something! Well, it won't be if you miss it.

The good news is that we can be sure we make the ultimate family reunion by believing and knowing Jesus Christ as Savior and Lord. And when we step over from this life to the next, He'll welcome us home with the greatest family reunion we can imagine.

I'm looking forward to that ultimate family reunion. I hope to see you there one day.

July 1

Professing to Be One Thing While Being Another

"Even so you too outwardly appear righteous to men,
but inwardly you are full of hypocrisy and lawlessness."
—**Matthew 23:28**

If you've been to China in the last few years, you know they have embraced capitalism with a passion while still professing to be communist. But professing to be one thing and doing another is not unique to communism in China. It's the case for many who call themselves Christians and yet live the way they want to live.

A recent Gallup poll found seventy-two percent of Americans believe that Jesus was the Son of God, yet eight percent feel each individual should arrive at his or her own beliefs independent of any church. Those two stats show a huge disconnect between belief and practice, between professing faith and living it. It's called hypocrisy and it's the number one reason people outside the church say they have no interest in Christianity.

Whether you're a communist or a Christian, practice what you preach—or at least have the integrity to call yourself something else. Actions reveal what you really believe, no matter how much you profess what you are.

July 2

SELF-MADE MAN

"The Lord favors those who fear Him,
those who wait for His lovingkindness."
—Psalm 147:11

There is no such thing as a self-made man. It's an American myth. The fact is, we are all indebted to someone.

Think about it. Most of you were born in America. Did you have any part in that decision? Did you write the Constitution that guarantees you freedom to live and work where you choose? Did you have anything to do with our nation's abundant natural resources?

What about the people who helped you along the way? Maybe it was a relative, a teacher, a coach, a friend, or a mentor. The fact is that no one can really call himself or herself self-made. We are all indebted to someone.

I urge you to take a few moments to say thanks to someone who has encouraged you along the way through a phone call, a note, or a visit. When you do, don't forget your Maker who has allowed you to be a part of this land we call America, the land of the free and the land of opportunity. God has blessed us through our land, and for that we can be forever grateful.

July 3

Pursuit of Happiness

"Do not be conformed to the this world,
but be transformed by the renewing of your mind . . ."
—Romans 12:2

In the Declaration of Independence, Thomas Jefferson tells us that all men are endowed by their Creator with certain unalienable rights: "life, liberty, and the pursuit of happiness." One thing's for sure, Americans have been pursuing happiness ever since . . . and with a passion!

However, I have bad news. If the pursuit of happiness is your primary goal, you'll never find it. Happiness is a by-product of being in God's will, and making the most of your gifts and talents. The pursuit of happiness is a selfish thing, and selfishness never leads to happiness.

Instead:

- Get to know God personally and begin to do His will.
- Live in a right relationship with Him and your fellow man.

Develop the gifts and abilities He's given you for His glory and for service to your fellow man. In the process, you may discover happiness. But pursuing happiness, well, you'll never find it that way. Pursue God in Christ, and happiness results.

July 4

SACRIFICED FOR YOUR FREEDOM

"It was for freedom that Christ set us free; therefore keep standing firm and do not be subject again to a yoke of slavery."
—**Galatians 5:1**

In 1776, George Washington gathered his troops together and told them he needed someone for a highly secret mission behind enemy lines. A twenty-one-year-old soldier from Yale volunteered. It seemed he was going to be successful, but as he returned with the battle plans of the British, they were tipped off and he was arrested and sentenced to be hanged. The next morning, as he was facing execution, he uttered these poignant words: "My only regret is that I have but one life to lose for my country."

This young man, Nathan Hale, was willing to pay a price for freedom that required his life. In many ways, what he did symbolized what Christ has done for all of us. Christ paid the ultimate price for our freedom from the bondage of sin. Freedom always involves a price—what Nathan Hale did for America and, likewise, what Jesus has done for us. Our choice is to accept it on faith with gratitude.

July 5

BORN TWICE

"Jesus answered and said to him, 'Truly, truly, I say to you, unless one is born again he cannot see the kingdom of God.'"
—John 3:3

There is a longing within everyone to be a part of a loving family that lasts. In a world of fractured marriages and dysfunctional families, that longing becomes greater. No matter what type of family we're from, God gives all of us a chance to be part of the only family that lasts. We had no choice on our earthly family, but we do have a choice on entering God's family through faith.

Jesus calls this spiritual birth the act of being born again. We all have a physical birthday, but not all of us have a spiritual birthday, which comes when we accept God's invitation to trust in Christ as Lord and Savior. With no spiritual birth, we die twice—physically and spiritually. But, with a spiritual birth, we die just once (physically,) for our spirit lives forever.

Born once, we die twice. Born twice, we die once.

If we're born twice, we're saved from spiritual death and we're in the family of God forever.

July 6

DOUBTS ABOUT GOD

"And He said to them, 'Where is your faith?'"
—Luke 8:25

Do you ever have doubts about God?
Most people do. Let me share with you what has caused me the most doubt through the years—the first four words of the Bible: "In the beginning God." I wonder, how could God always exist? Where did He come from? What did He do before creation?

But "In the beginning God" also enriches my faith. For the Bible also says, "In the beginning was the Word and the Word was God and the Word became flesh." The Word is Jesus Christ and because of Jesus' life, I can see what God is like. Because of His death I can see and experience His love. Because the evidence of His resurrection is overwhelming, I can believe in God's power to do anything.

If Jesus rose from the dead, I can live with the questions I can't understand about God—like His always existing—because He is God and I'm not. We all have doubts about God, but Jesus is the reason I can believe in God.

July 7

SETBACK INTO COMEBACK

"But in all these things we overwhelmingly conquer
through Him who loved us."
—Romans 8:37

If ever there is a modern day hero, it's Lance Armstrong, who won his seventh straight Tour de France in July 2005. Can you imagine biking over 2,000 miles on some of the steepest roads in the world—the Alps? Those cyclists are tough!

What makes Armstrong such a hero is that in 1996, he learned he had cancer with not much of a chance to survive. But he battled and overcame it so dramatically that he won perhaps the most grueling physical challenge in sports. He turned a setback into a comeback. What a hero!

How about you? What setbacks are you facing in your life? A key to victorious living is learning how to turn a setback into a comeback. I believe faith in God is a tremendous help in doing so. Ask God to help you transform your setback into a comeback. And when you do, you'll become a hero and inspiration to many around you.

July 8

MARITAL SEX

"I am my beloved's and my beloved is mine . . ."
—Song of Solomon 6:3

Do you realize how positive the Bible is about sex in marriage? Listen to God's Word: "The husband should fulfill his marital duty to his wife and, likewise, the wife to her husband." God's Word goes on: "The wife's body does not belong to her alone but also to her husband."

You'd expect that in words written in the first century A.D., but listen to the radical teaching that follows: "In the same way, the husband's body does not belong to him alone but also to his wife." That was radical, counter-cultural teaching for the patriarchal first century.

But God's Word applies to every age. It will always be counter-cultural in certain ways. Today, it's radically counter-cultural to teach that sex in marriage is the best. There is tremendous freedom for the husband and wife to enjoy one another. Our bodies are for the pleasure of our spouse exclusively, no one else. That's radical, but it's best. So trust the Inventor of sex to know best.

July 9

TROUBLE

"I, even I, am He who comforts you."
—Isaiah 51:12

Corporate downsizing. Rebellious teenagers. An unfaithful spouse. A devastating illness. Life often brings trouble our way. Sometimes we are so overwhelmed we struggle to merely stay afloat.

Difficulty during times of trouble should come as no surprise to students of the Bible. Jesus Christ said in John 16:33, "In this world you will have problems." That doesn't sound like a very optimistic outlook. However, He goes on to say, "But take heart! I have overcome the world." That message is positive indeed.

Trouble. Difficulty. These things are a reality in this life. Jesus Christ promises us that He has provided victory over those things which cause us so much pain. Trusting in Him is the key to overcoming these problems.

Why not evaluate your present struggles from a biblical perspective—from Christ's perspective? You have nothing to lose and everything to gain!

July 10

SMORGASBORD RELIGION

"Beloved, do not believe every spirit,
but test the spirits to see whether they are from God,
because many false prophets have gone out into the world."
—1 John 4:1

It is so trendy to practice smorgasbord religion: a little dose of Jesus, a little pinch of Buddha, a little Mohammed here and a little New Age thought there. It makes you sound so with it—so spiritual.

But it is fundamentally dishonest. It is an insult to each religion. It is like spiritual looting. It is classic refashioning of God into your own chic image; it is a reminder of the many intellectual airheads today. Make a decision! But don't be a phony for every faith. They don't say the same things, they don't believe the same things.

Jesus said, "I am the way, the truth, the life. No one comes to the Father but through Me." Either He lied, was terribly insane, or is Who He said He is. This is in direct conflict with every other religion. With Him, it's all or nothing. I believe He is the truth about God.

Make a decision about Jesus, Mohammed, Buddha, or whomever. But don't insult them all with this airhead pseudo-sophisticated practice of smorgasbord religion.

July 11

GOD'S CLOCK

". . . with the Lord one day is like a thousand years,
and a thousand years like one day."
—2 Peter 3:8

Have you ever thought about how God doesn't see time as you and I do? The Bible tells us that to God, one day is as 1000 years, and 1000 years are as one day. He sees the past, present, and future all at once—for He is over time. That blows my mind. We are so finite. We begin. We end. God always was, is, and will be. Isn't that amazing?

When we get to heaven, there will be no clocks and no calendars. It will be timeless. That unsettles me. Clocks and calendars bring order to my life. A place with no time just boggles my mind. But we'll never be tired, and that will be great!

Even though God is over time, at the perfect time He became one of us, as a baby boy. He invaded history right on time—BC/AD—it was the zero hour, to show us Himself, save us from sin, and offer us eternal life with Him. Timeless life. Isn't that amazing? Won't you take *time* to consider this?

July 12

Is Wealth Worth It?

"No one can serve two masters; for either he will hate the one and love the other, or he will be devoted to one and despise the other. You cannot serve God and wealth."
—Matthew 6:24

What amount of money separates you from happiness? Is it a raise, or winning millions in the lottery? It is a common misconception that man can find contentment in money.

John D. Rockefeller, at one time the world's richest man, was asked, "How many millions would it take for you to be satisfied?" He replied, "The next one."

That's a clear example of how the pursuit of money can become such a preeminent concern that it creates an insatiable appetite, making us never satisfied with what we have.

Jesus said, ". . . man cannot serve God and money." That's tough. Can't we serve them both? The answer is no. Jesus teaches that if we don't choose God, we'll become slaves to our desire for money and possessions. One course ends in futility and bondage, and the other in fulfillment and freedom for living. Choose Christ and He will fully meet your needs. You will find riches beyond anything you possess.

WISDOM OF GOD VS. WISDOM OF MAN

"The fear of the LORD is the beginning of wisdom;
a good understanding have all those who do
His commandments."
—Psalm 111:10

Have you ever thought about mankind's endless search for truth in this world? Think about it. Even in the twenty-first century, a time of the greatest knowledge in the history of man, with all the technological developments that have accelerated the rate of acquiring knowledge, the restless mind of man still struggles with discovering the reason for his existence.

Part of the trouble results from looking for that answer through worldly wisdom versus godly wisdom. Worldly wisdom leaves you empty and a bit cynical, but godly wisdom is different. It reveals to us ultimate truth, and that truth is found in a person . . . Jesus Christ. Take time to pursue ultimate truth in the person of Jesus and in the teachings of His Word, the Bible, and you will find wisdom that is out of this world. Discover the wisdom of God over the wisdom of the world, and in the process you will have discovered your answer for life. I promise you, this is the truth.

July 14

Eternal Life

"... for unless you believe that I am He,
you will die in your sins."
—John 8:24

The late baseball great Ted Williams and his son paid a company $136,000 to store Ted's body in liquid nitrogen so that when science discovers a way to beat death, his frozen body will be ready to claim the cure. Sometimes wealthy people without God go to bizarre extremes to have a shot at beating death. So far no scheme has worked.

But I have good news. One man *has* beaten death and He offers us the key to victory over death, and eternal life. It won't cost you a nickel, but you have to be willing to entrust your life to His hands. You have to believe He is God, the One who became a man to die for your sins—who rose from the dead. In short, you have to entrust your life to Jesus alone for victory over death.

Otherwise, it's no deal and death wins. Jesus has exclusive rights to victory over death. Trust Him and claim the victory.

July 15

PARENTING TEENS ISN'T EASY

*"And Jesus kept increasing in wisdom and stature,
and in favor with God and men."*
—**Luke 2:52**

M ark Twain said, "When a child turns thirteen, put them in a barrel and feed them through a hole. When they get to be sixteen, plug up the hole." That's not a very positive view of parenting teens, but one that everyone can relate to. Parenting teens isn't easy.

David Gelman writes, "Today's teenagers face more adult-type stresses than their predecessors did, at a time when adults are much less available to help them." So here are a few suggestions:

- *Education is not the goal, wisdom is.* Education helps, but teaching kids to sort out information is the key.
- *Teach them how to take care of their bodies with a good diet and good exercise.* And remember—safe sex isn't safe . . . only abstinence is.
- *Help them develop a relationship with God.* Recognize that much of their development will come from the relationship with God they see in you.
- *Teach them that there are moral absolutes based on Scripture.* Teens need these guidelines.
- *Help them make wise decisions about the company they keep.* Positive peer pressure is key.
- *Pray*—Teens and parents of teens need lots of prayer!

July 16

FAITHFULNESS

"He who is faithful in a very little thing
is faithful also in much . . ."
—Luke 16:10

I don't know many qualities more appreciated than faithfulness. Faithfulness is about dependability, loyalty, trustworthiness, and consistency.

Faithful people are faithful all the time—not most of the time. I've been married over thirty years. That's over 10,950 days. How do you think my wife would feel if I prided myself on being faithful to her 10,949 days? She wouldn't be happy. Just one day of unfaithfulness can ruin all the days of faithfulness, because faithfulness means being faithful all the time.

The longer I live, the more I appreciate people who are faithful; especially those who are faithful to God. That leads them to be faithful to their spouse, parents, brothers, sisters, friends, church members, co-workers, those with whom they serve in a ministry or an organization. The longer we live, the more we appreciate faithfulness.

July 17

How Can God Be Three in One?

".... God sent forth His Son, born of a woman ... that we might receive the adoption as sons. Because you are sons, God has sent forth the Spirit of His Son into our hearts ...."
—Galatians 4:4–6

How can God be three-in-one ... Father, Son, *and* Holy Spirit? This belief is central to Christianity.

Some argue that Christianity teaches belief in three Gods, or polytheism. Not true. Christianity, like Judaism and Islam, is rigidly monotheistic. Yet Judaism and Islam do not believe God is three in one. No other religion does.

I can try to explain by saying I'm a father to my three sons—they know me one way. I'm a son of my parents—they know me another way. I'm the husband of my wife—she knows me another way. Three roles, but all the same person.

That may help, but it's still inadequate. For how do we explain God the Son, praying to God the Father, as Jesus did? It is unexplainable to the human mind, because we are not God. The Trinity will always be a mystery that reflects the unfathomable greatness of God. Yet, when you believe, you begin to know the fullness of God.

July 18

SHEEP OR GOATS

"... I will show you my faith by my works."
—James 2:18

Jesus says that when He comes again all mankind will be divided into two camps—the sheep and the goats. The sheep are in His eternal kingdom. The goats are not. He says the sheep feed the hungry, clothe the needy, and care for those who are sick and in prison. Does this mean we get to heaven by good works? Absolutely not! God's Word says, "For by God's grace we are saved through faith, and not of ourselves. It is a gift of God, not as a result of works."

What Jesus is saying is that true faith always *results* in good works, especially to the needy. We can't do it all, but the church can. When we have saving faith and begin to give and serve through a local church, we take part in all types of ministries as a part of the body of Christ.

If Jesus comes today, which group will you be in—His sheep, or the Devil's goats?

July 19

SEX AND SEXUALITY

"Nor let us act immorality, as some of them did . . ."
—1 Corinthians 10:8

On a recent trip to Eastern Europe, I went to workout in the fitness center. Two of the five TVs were parked on MTV and VH1, with beautiful, half-naked seductive dancers. I then went to breakfast, and a large flat-screen TV was the central focus, as American music videos with more beautiful, scantily clad dancers filled the screen. Our waiter was so entranced I couldn't even get a cup of coffee.

The dominant export of American culture, in the name of freedom, is our entertainment industry; freedom to do what you want rather than freedom with responsibility, honor, and character. We're assaulted 24/7 with sex and sexuality, and we're exporting it around the world.

But God had a different idea when He invented sex: it was designed by God to be enjoyed between a man and woman to the fullest in marriage. God's idea is still the best. It's radically counter-cultural and it takes great faith and courage to live it out. Yet God's plan for sex is unmatched. All others are counterfeits.

July 20

Sexual Freedom

"Stop depriving one another . . ."
—1 Corinthians 7:5

Sexual freedom is an obsession for many. But God, the inventor of sex, tells us the best kind of sexual freedom is found in marriage. Listen to His Word: "The wife does not have authority over her own body, but the husband does, and likewise also the husband does not have authority over his own body." These words were radical for the first century and they're still radical today.

This concept of mutual submission leads to tremendous sexual freedom between a husband and wife. It also teaches us that husbands and wives should take care of their bodies—not just for the Lord, and not just for their health—but, also, for the enjoyment of their spouses.

Note that the key words are *between a husband and wife*. All other sexual intimacy is out of bounds. Sex outside of marriage is simply not what the Inventor of sex had in mind. Remember, God's way is the best way to true sexual freedom.

DEFINITION OF SUCCESS

"Only be strong and very courageous; be careful to do according
to all the law which Moses My servant commanded you;
do not turn from it to the right or to the left,
so that you may have success wherever you go."
—Joshua 1:7

How do we become a lasting success and what would that definition be?

Ann Landers, the great guru of newspaper advice, once wrote, "To a great many people, money is a measure of success. If they are living on a lavish scale, they think they are successes. And yet many are dismal failures."

Og Mandino, the author of *The Greatest Salesman in the World,* says, "The only difference between success and failure is good and bad habits—success is a state of mind."

What is your definition of success? Let me suggest this one: Success is the process of fulfilling your purpose in life and doing it well. In short, success is a by-product of a life well lived.

I propose to you that the most successful person who ever lived is Jesus Christ. He knew His purpose: To reveal God to us in a person, and to offer Himself as our Savior by dying for our sins. He fulfilled it perfectly. Jesus Christ was the most successful man who ever walked this earth. Look to Him in faith. He'll put you on the road to success—God's way.

July 22

LET THE GOOD TIMES ROLL

". . . 'Come now, I will test you with pleasure . . .
it too was futility."
—Ecclesiastes 2:1

Jerry Seinfeld, that famous philosopher of the nineties, has said, "Everybody is looking for good sex, good food, and a good laugh because they are little islands of relief in what's often a very painful existence." Does that describe you?

Constantly seeking pleasure will mean finding life empty and unfulfilling. Look at the gurus of pleasure, such as Madonna, now a mother, and Hugh Hefner, who tried marriage and having children. Obviously, their actions speak volumes about the fact that pursuit of pleasure alone does not bring the sense of fulfillment in life that so many desire.

Here's the shocker—seeking pleasure without God always leads to emptiness and futility. To really experience joy and fulfillment of living, we have to plant both feet firmly with God. Trust Him and do things His way. It's the key to enjoying life!

HONOR MOM AND DAD

"Honor your father and your mother . . ."
—Exodus 20:12

One of the more important commandments of God is to "Honor thy father and mother." It is lived out in three phases of the parent-child relationship:

1. When a child is growing up in the home, he is called to obey. Parents have to teach their children to obey, and children honor their parents through obedience.
2. The second phase begins when the children become young adults. They aren't as dependent on their parents and are no longer called to obey, but to respect their parents. This is usually the longest phase.
3. The third phase is to honor parents by caring for them in their old age when they are no longer able to care for themselves. This is a tough transition, when children become parents to their parents.

Obedience, respect, and care—the three stages of honoring Mom and Dad. The welfare of the family is dependent on our obeying God's command.

July 24

THE INVITATION

"Behold, I stand at the door and knock;
if anyone hears My voice and opens the door,
I will come in to him . . ."
—Revelation 3:20

I don't know whether you've ever been invited to the White House or have ever been asked to make an appearance at Buckingham Palace, but wouldn't it be amazing to have the President of the United States or the Queen of England desire to visit your home? Even more amazing, there is a King who represents royalty and power greater than anyone who desires to do just that.

The Bible tells us that it's Jesus Christ, the King of kings. Jesus talks about our life like it's a home. He says He is standing outside the door of our life, knocking and hoping we'll invite Him in. If you do open the door and invite Him in, He promises to enter. When He comes into your life, He brings meaning, companionship, love, and strength to face the demands of life. He brings everything you need to live a complete, purposeful life.

How about it? Why not open the door today and you can have dinner with the King of kings, forever and ever.

WINDOW WASHER

"For the LORD will be your confidence . . ."
—Proverbs 3:26

Have you ever looked up and noticed window washers at work on a skyscraper? Why do you suppose they can work so confidently suspended so high above the ground? They are secure because they know their safety harnesses are fastened to the building and their harnesses will hold even if the platform should fall.

Your life can be lived on the edge, with confidence like that. When we give our lives to Jesus Christ, He becomes our safety and our security. Because of Him, we can risk living life to the fullest and be all that we were created to be. He keeps us secure, even though life is often insecure, even though we get disappointed, even though the bottom falls out.

How about you? Do you have security for today, no matter what challenges and dangers you face? How about tomorrow?

Why not try living life with Christ one day at a time for a life that's secure and yet full of excitement.

July 26

Dad's Greatest Priorities

". . . 'Who are these with you?' So he said,
'The children whom God has graciously given your servant.'"
—Genesis 33:5

Let's take a moment to remember the Bible's three greatest priorities for dads:

1. *Husbands, love your wives* (Ephesians 5:25). The best way to be a good father is to be a loving husband. Our children need that more than anything. Remember, the biblical word for love means more than a feeling, it means a commitment.

2. *Fathers, do not provoke your children to anger* (Ephesians 6:4). Every child's psyche is fragile. We can expect too much at times and come down too hard. Worst of all, we can shut out our kids emotionally. We should build them up, and not destroy the spirit and self-image of our children.

3. *Bring them up in the discipline and instruction of the Lord* (Ephesians 6:4). We need to be godly men who know the Book, who live it, and teach it to our kids. Kids need to know their boundaries. It gives them security. They also need to be taught right from wrong.

To sum it up, the best fathers love their wives, their kids, and the Lord. Fathers, may this be our goal every day.

July 27

KNOW THYSELF

"... that I may know Him and the power of His resurrection ..."
—Philippians 3:10

The person we spend the most time with is our *self,* so we tend to be pretty interested in ourselves. Question. Do you really like yourself? Would you rather be somebody else? Are you realistic about your strengths and weaknesses?

Socrates gets credit for saying, "Know thyself," even though what he really said, was, "The unexamined life is not worth living." Either way, the message is clear. Knowing ourselves is a key to a meaningful life.

Let me go a step further. Since God is your Creator and He knows you better than anyone else, why don't you get to know God personally; then you'll get to know yourself—the real you—better than you ever could on your own. God gives us the way to know Him through Jesus and His Word. If you get to know Him, you'll come to know yourself and why you're here. You'll be on the road to a very meaningful life.

July 28

Understanding Our Wives

"Who among you is wise and understanding? Let him show
by his good behavior his deeds in the gentleness of wisdom."
—James 3:13

It had been a fun day of vacation. I had gotten up early and jogged on the beach, joined some friends for a round of golf, had time for a couple of sets of tennis and finished off the day with a refreshing swim in the ocean. After showering and dressing for dinner, I happily exclaimed to my wife, "Man! It's been a great day!" But the look she gave me was not filled with love. You see, our boys were young—one still in diapers. In classic "airhead husband style," I had been oblivious to the needs of my wife.

God's Word says, "Husbands, live with your wives in an understanding way." We don't naturally understand our wives' needs when we are wrapped up in our own little world. Understanding means love, unselfishness, compassionate listening without giving advice, partnering in parenting, and much, much more.

Men, ask God to help you be what you just can't be on your own—understanding of your wife.

THE NEW NUMBER ONE OBJECTION TO CHRISTIANITY

"He who is of God hears the words of God . . ."
—John 8:47

In the last twenty years, a new number-one objection to Christianity has emerged: "Why do Christians think they have the only way to God and heaven?" In our pluralistic world, this is hard to take. In a world of tolerance, this seems intolerable.

But here's the problem: Jesus said, "I am the way, the truth, the life. *No one* comes to the Father but through Me." Was Jesus really that narrow-minded and egocentric? A natural question, but the wrong question.

The key question: "Was He telling the truth?" If He wasn't, we certainly don't want to believe in Him. But if He was, you might have a problem with that if you feel there are many ways to heaven. You would be calling Jesus a liar . . . and saying that He is wrong. Your problem is really with Jesus, more than with Christians who believe Him.

What do you believe? Do you believe Jesus tells the truth? That's the decision we must deal with if we are open and honest.

July 30

BACK IN CHURCH

"... AS I LIVE, SAYS THE LORD, EVERY KNEE SHALL BOW TO ME, AND EVERY TONGUE SHALL GIVE PRAISE TO GOD."
—Romans 14:11

Will it take six strong men to get you back in church again? Six strong men to carry your body in a casket down the aisle?

The church is a place to worship, to be encouraged, to be spiritually rejuvenated, and a place to learn what it means to have a true relationship with God. There's no perfect church because there are no perfect people. And imperfect people need God and the forgiveness and salvation He offers in Jesus. I encourage you to find a church. If six strong men have to carry you there, it will be too late.

July 31

WATER IN THE DESERT

". . . the water that I will give him will become in him
a well of water springing up to eternal life."
—John 4:14

If you've ever traveled through the desert, you'll notice that it's mile after mile of dry and barren landscape. Then suddenly, there's a spot of green, some trees, bushes, and flowering plants. It always means there's some kind of water source nearby. With water, the desert blossoms and comes to life.

The same is true in our lives. Without God, we tend to dry up when life gets hard. It saps us of all our energy, creativity, and drive. We eventually feel beaten down, worn out, and dried up. But Jesus says, "I am living water; anyone who accepts Me will never be thirsty again." He wasn't talking about physical thirst. He was talking about satisfying our spiritual thirst so we can blossom and come to life.

What about it? Do you sometimes feel like a dry, dusty shrub in a desert of emptiness? Come to Christ and enjoy a cool drink of water whenever you need it.

August 1

TRIALS

"Blessed is a man who perseveres under trial; for once he has been approved, he will receive the crown of life . . ."
—James 1:12

There's an Arab proverb that goes like this: "All sunshine makes for a desert." Have you ever thought of life that way?

All of us want things to go our way all the time, but we have to admit that life doesn't work like that. Hard times come. Relationships are damaged. Financial worries plague us. There are even times of war. Yes, the clouds and the storms really do come.

Jesus said, "In this world, you will have trouble." But the good news is, He didn't stop there. He also said, "Take heart. I have overcome the world." Yes, trouble is a fact of life. But Jesus has given us a means of finding victory—the real victory—even in hard times.

Won't you allow Him to provide all you need to face the good times and the bad? He's willing and able to provide triumph, even when things look the darkest. Put your trust in Jesus Christ.

August 2

Do Not Disturb

"... do not merely look out for your own personal interests,
but also for the interests of others."
—Philippians 2:4

When it comes to serving our fellow man, most of us tend to live with a mindset that posts a "Do Not Disturb" sign over our hearts. We think, "I'm too busy. Leave me alone. I don't want to get involved. I've got my own agenda . . ."

Our culture is overrun with the attitude, "It's all about me." But as Rick Warren writes in his best seller, *The Purpose Driven Life,* "A meaningful life begins when we realize it's not all about us. It's all about God." When we get to know our Creator through Jesus Christ, and begin to worship God and serve Him, we realize the way we serve God is to serve our fellow man—especially those in need.

"It's all about me" is incredibly selfish, and it leads to emptiness and spiritual death. Real living begins when we start to know God and serve Him. Serving God means serving others. It's one of the keys to discovering your life purpose.

August 3

ABSOLUTE TRUTH

"You will know the truth, and the truth will make you free."
—John 8:32

Is there such a thing as absolute truth?
Most Americans say there isn't. A recent study showed that seventy-one percent of American adults believe there is no such thing as absolute truth. To most of them, truth is relative—relative to their own situation. This means people are creating their own personal moral code, which can be a recipe for disaster. When truth is relative, absolutely anything seems OK.

So is there absolute truth?

Absolutely! But it's not found in a religion, a philosophy, or in the ever-changing world of science. It's found in a person—Jesus Christ. Jesus said, "I am the way, the truth, the life." He is the way to God, the truth about right and wrong, and the key to abundant life.

Do you want to know absolute truth? Look to Jesus Christ in God's Word. Do you want to know how to live the truth? Just look and see what Jesus did.

August 4

CRISIS OF SUCCESS

".. . To Him be the glory forever."
—Romans 11:36

Stephen Berglas in *The Success Syndrome—Hitting Bottom When You Reach the Top* writes about the crisis of success. He says one major cause is "encore anxiety" or fear that you won't be able to repeat or sustain earlier achievements. So here are a few thoughts to consider as you pursue success:

- The price of success is not just hard work and sacrifice, but the crisis you face when success finally comes. Some are dumbfounded by the emptiness they feel when goals are achieved.
- With the privileges of success comes a greater sense of responsibility.
- Surprisingly, the toughest challenge to a person's character is not adversity, but how one deals with the privileges and pressures of success.

So why seek it? God wants us to make the most of *our* talents for *His* glory. And that's the key: *His* glory, not ours. When we earn it and make the most of it God's way, we realize it's the only way to truly enjoy success.

August 5

JESUS' MISSION

"For even the Son of Man did not come to be served, but to serve,
and to give His life as a ransom for many."
—Mark 10:45

Imagine that news from Al Jazeera television shows some American soldiers captured by terrorists in the Middle East. The report is grim—they face death within a few days. The Chairman of the Joint Chiefs of Staff sees the story from America. He orders a mobilization of a rescue mission to find these men. But what shocks those around him is that he will lead the mission himself. He leaves the comfort of his safe office in the Pentagon and flies to the Middle East.

Amazingly, the mission is a success. The men are set free but, sadly, one man on the mission is killed—the Chairman of the Joint Chiefs of Staff. He gave his life to deliver those in captivity from evil.

That's what the story of Jesus is all about. He left all the comfort and power of heaven to go on a mission to liberate us from the captivity of the evil one and sin. Are you willing to let Jesus set you free to really live life to the fullest? Do you believe it?

August 6

EVIDENCE FOR THE RESURRECTION

"Now on the first day of the week Mary Magdalene came early
to the tomb . . . and saw the stone already taken away . . ."
—John 20:1

What evidence is there for the resurrection of Jesus Christ? First of all, the church still exists to this day. Do you realize that only one fact—the resurrection of Jesus—gave the early church its power? But when Jesus died on the cross, His followers left Him and fled for their lives; yet something occurred to empower them with great faith.

People continue to experience the risen Christ living in them, and Sunday is now the day of worship. How else can you explain a group of Jewish people, who revered the Sabbath, changing the day of worship from Saturday to Sunday? Sunday became known as the Lord's Day, because Jesus rose from the dead that day.

If the resurrection doesn't account for this, what does? I realize this is not proof of the resurrection, but it is evidence for believing the resurrection.

August 7

DIVORCE PREVENTION

"'For I hate divorce,' says the LORD . . ."
—Malachi 2:16

Everybody likes to be thought of as number one! America is a nation that prides itself on being number one in many categories, but we are number one in a category that is not good—we're number one in divorce. One out of every two marriages ends in divorce.

When Jesus was asked about divorce, He made it clear that it was never what God had in mind. He quickly began to talk about marriage and the commitment that's involved. Obviously, a marriage that lasts a lifetime is what God desires. Let me suggest twelve words for you and your spouse to live by; words that help with divorce prevention:

- I love you.
- I admire you.
- I was wrong.
- Please forgive me.

Expressing love and admiration, admitting when we are wrong and asking forgiveness are the ingredients for divorce prevention. Wouldn't it be great if, one day, America became number one in marriages that last!

August 8

True Faith Lived Out

". . . THE RIGHTEOUS MAN SHALL LIVE BY FAITH."
—Galatians 3:11

Many centuries ago, God revealed how true faith is lived out. God's Word says, "What does the Lord require of you but to do justice, to love kindness, and to walk humbly with your God."

Think about it. Doing justice is to be concerned for those who are left out, overlooked, abused, and oppressed. To love kindness is being considerate, thoughtful, and actively working for the good of others. Walking humbly with God is seeing God and self from the right perspective, thankful for His grace.

Today, when it seems that religious faith is seen as negative and even bigoted, I hope you will consider God's Word. Only one person in all of history has lived up to this standard, and that was Jesus Christ. He alone was just and kind and walked with His Father, God. He can help you live out life today as a demonstration of what true faith is. Why not try it?

August 9

OBJECTION:
THE BIBLE IS FULL OF ERRORS

"For the word of God is living and active and sharper than any two-edged sword, and piercing as far as the division of soul and spirit . . . and able to judge the thoughts and intentions of the heart."
—Hebrews 4:12

One of the main objections to Christianity: "The Bible is filled with myths and mistakes. It's a book of men rather than a book of God." But the real questions behind this objection are:

- Can the Bible be trusted?
- Is it really true?
- Is it God's word, or man's?

First response: What mistakes are you concerned about? Is there a possibility you are parroting some professor, like the breathtaking brilliance of a college freshman? Or, have you really studied it yourself and determined there are mistakes?

Secondly, all of Scripture's dependability rises and falls with the resurrection of Jesus Christ. If that did not occur, the book is filled with lies and Christianity is a colossal hoax! But if Jesus rose from the dead, then everything else in the Bible is possible and believable. Believing the Bible begins with Jesus. And faith in Jesus begins with the trustworthiness of Scripture.

August 10

PARENTING CHILDREN

*"You shall teach them to your sons, talking of them when you sit
. . . when you walk . . . when you lie down and
when you rise up."*
—Deuteronomy 11:19

The first stage of parenting children in the home begins with the preschool years. The second stage is the childhood years, ages six through twelve. During these years, parents should practice the baton principle: in a relay race, the most important time is the passing of the baton. If it's dropped, the race is lost. Parenting children in the home means passing the baton of godly values to the next generation.

God's Word teaches us as parents to love God with all our hearts, souls, and might, and to diligently teach the commands of God to our children when we sit in our house, when we walk by the way, when we lie down, and when we rise up. We need to teach our kids how to live as we go about everyday life; in short, our kids need to see that our faith in God is real and consistent. This calls for a lot of love for God and for our children. But, when done well, the baton of godly values is handed to the new generation.

August 11

AGING PARENTS

"'HONOR YOUR FATHER AND MOTHER' (which is the first commandment with a promise) . . ."
—Ephesians 6:2

Perhaps the toughest stage in life is parenting our parents. It's a role reversal both parent and child would rather avoid. The Bible clearly teaches us to honor our parents, and that means caring for them when they are old. Let me suggest a few thoughts:

- The greatest gift you can give your aging parents is time, but if physical distance is great, take time to call or write on a regular basis.
- Be prayerful and sensitive when parents can no longer care for themselves or their home. Be honest in helping them think about where they'll live—be it a retirement center, a nursing home, or with you.
- As you face these tough decisions, be motivated by love—not guilt. Do what they most need, not what you most want.

Honoring our parents sometimes means parenting our parents. Remember, we reap what we sow. One day, we hope that our children will have learned from us how to care for us when we are old.

GOOD NEWS IN A WORLD OF BAD NEWS

". . . I came that they might have life, and have it abundantly."
—John 10:10

We're constantly bombarded with bad news on newscast after newscast. It's depressing. The harsh reality of the daily news challenges those who believe that man is inherently good and the world is getting better.

The Bible tells us the truth. Human beings are not innately good and kind, and society is not progressing toward universal peace and harmony. Just the opposite is true. Man's sin is a constant reality and if we don't want to believe it, we can just ignore the news and refuse to lock our doors at night.

There is good news, however. God is in control of history and anyone who acknowledges a need for God in Christ holds the key to inner peace and security. In Christ, whether we live or die, we can't lose. Christ gives us the key to eternal life and living this life victoriously.

August 13

KEY TO GREATNESS

*"Then He poured water into the basin,
and began to wash the disciples' feet . . ."*
—John 13:5

When you think of someone who is truly great, who do you think of?

You might think of Bach or Beethoven. Maybe you think of President Washington or Lincoln. Talents, accomplishments, power, fame, or wealth, usually determine greatness in this world. But Jesus tells us the true measurement of greatness in the kingdom of God is the kind of servant you are. He healed the sick. He reached out to the hurting. He even washed His disciples' feet. In the end, His greatest service was to give His life as a ransom for many.

The late Al Burruss said, "When you're alive, your wealth is measured by the number who serve you. But when you die, your wealth is measured by the number that you've served." Jesus is the greatest example of that truth. He served us all.

Do you want to be great? Jesus set the ultimate example by serving us to the point of the ultimate personal sacrifice. Why don't you seek to be great by being a servant to your fellow man?

August 14

THREE KEYS FOR MOM

"... rejoicing in hope, persevering in tribulation,
devoted to prayer ..."
—Romans 12:12

It's not easy being a mom these days. Whether you're home full-time, or working outside the home, there are challenges. There's a verse in Romans that contains three keys for moms:

Be joyful in hope. Every mom has hope for her kids. When a mom trusts in the Lord and believes His promises in Scripture, she can be joyful in hope for the future of her family.

Persevere in trials. There will be difficulties and trials for every mom (kids not doing well, times of feeling unappreciated, etc.). But when her hope is grounded in God, she can find strength to endure any trial.

Be devoted to prayer. Hey, moms, with so many trials and so much out of your control, be devoted to prayer. Turn your concerns, your fears, and your children over to the Lord. Prayer is the power source for being a great mom and a great person.

Hope, perseverance, and prayer—three keys to victory for moms.

August 15

THE ANTICHRIST

"For false Christs and false prophets will arise and will show
great signs and wonders, so as to mislead,
if possible, even the elect."
—**Matthew 24:24**

Who is the most charismatic leader you've ever seen—past or present. Is it a political leader, religious leader, a leader in academia? Leaders can be a tremendous influence for good or evil.

The Bible talks about a great leader who will burst onto the world scene. He will appear to be good, seeking to bring unity and peace to the world. He will focus on the desire for economic prosperity. He will be an extraordinarily brilliant and gifted leader who will cause the world to be in awe.

But don't be led astray. The Bible calls him the Antichrist. He will be incredibly attractive and charismatic, but it will be "all about himself." He will be the embodiment of evil, but appear to be good. He will be an imposter and a counterfeit of the one Man who will ultimately bring true peace—Jesus Christ. That's why this man is called the Antichrist. Study what the Bible says about the contrast of the *Anti*christ and Jesus. Believe, and don't be deceived.

August 16

LETTING GO AS A PARENT

*"I have no greater joy than this,
to hear of my children walking in the truth."*
—3 John 1:4

There was an emotional moment my wife and I experienced with all of our boys. It happened when we walked each of them to the bus stop to begin first grade, knowing the first stage of parenting (the preschool years) was over.

Then it happened again as each of our boys left home for college. Really, the whole parenting process is one of letting go. Let me make a few suggestions:

1. Do whatever you can to allow Mom to be at home full-time with the children in the preschool years. I realize single parents don't have this option, but if you can work it out, do it. This short-term sacrifice brings long-term results.
2. Love them always, and let them *know* of your love for them.
3. Discipline them consistently, so that they'll know there are consequences for stepping over the line.
4. Pray for them regularly, that they'll make wise choices and that their influences are for good.

Letting go is not easy, but with God's help and our love, our children can grow to be responsible adults.

August 17

Ethics and Morality

"Many will say to Me on that day, 'Lord, Lord' . . . and I will declare to them, 'I never knew you; DEPART FROM ME, YOU WHO PRACTICE LAWLESSNESS.'"
—Matthew 7:22–23

The *New York Times* ran a front-page article on the lives of strippers in Las Vegas. It seems they have heated up the controversy on stripper etiquette and whether it is right or wrong for them to engage in prostitution. One stripper even said she would never engage in prostitution because she "had God in her life." I wonder what God thinks of that.

We all have moral values, but are they the right moral values? The fact is, everyone has a moral philosophy, some code of right and wrong. Most believe passionately in their code—even the Mafia. In ancient Israel when the people turned from God, the Bible says each man did what was right in his own eyes. That is America today where all kinds of evil are rationalized. God may be given lip service, but His Word on morality is ignored.

The greatest moral philosophy is found in Jesus and in God's Word. Ignore this and you'll be amazed at what you'll find yourself justifying.

August 18

TOUGH PRESSURE ON THE FAMILY

"But seek first His kingdom and His righteousness,
and all these things will be added to you."
—Matthew 6:33

One of the toughest pressures working against the family is materialism. Kids keep the pressure on parents to have what their friends have. Husbands put pressure on their wives to go to work—to keep up with the Jones family, though she may prefer to be at home. Wives often make it clear to husbands how dissatisfied they are with what they have, causing the husband to feel like an unappreciated failure. To top it all off, Madison Avenue adds fuel to the fire by convincing us every product is the gateway to happiness. Materialism, often rationalized as a concern for the family, has a way, unfortunately, of creating enormous dissatisfaction within the family.

Jesus has a better idea which almost seems un-American in our culture of consumerism: "Seek first His kingdom and His righteousness [as described in the Bible] and all *these* things shall be added unto you." Does that mean we don't work hard? Absolutely not! We are called to work, but it has to do with priorities that help the family stay together.

God unites the family. Materialism pulls it apart.

August 19

WHO DO YOU THINK JESUS IS?

"[Jesus] said to them, 'But who do you say that I am?'"
—Matthew 16:15

In our increasingly secular and biblically illiterate culture, there are all sorts of ideas about who Jesus is. For many weeks in 2003, *The DaVinci Code,* by Dan Brown, was a number one bestseller. It described Jesus as just a man who was married to Mary Magdalene. It said they had a child, and the church sought to cover this up for 2,000 years. The book appeals to pseudo-intellectuals who have weak historical and biblical backgrounds.

Who do *you* think Jesus is? That's the question Jesus asked His disciples. Peter replied, "You are the Christ, the Son of the Living God." Jesus affirmed his answer.

Most of the world accepts Jesus, the man, as a good prophet or teacher. But only a minority of the world believes He is "the Christ, the son of the Living God." I'm part of the minority who believe Jesus is who He says He is. What about you? Who do *you* think Jesus is?

Jesus and Church Hypocrites

*"But you, when you pray, go into your inner room,
close your door and pray to your Father who is in secret,
and your Father who sees what is done in secret
will reward you."*
—Matthew 6:6

One of the main objections to Christianity and the church is all the hypocrisy. No doubt, there's a ton of it. Most people outside the church don't realize how much Jesus hates hypocrisy as well. In His most famous sermon He blasted showy giving and praying that was designed to impress others rather than to please God and help our fellow man.

He says the best way to give to others is to do it anonymously. The best way to pray is to seek a place to be alone with God and privately pour out your heart to Him.

It's not that Jesus is down on doing good publicly; it's the motive that matters. One thing is for sure: showy religious hypocrites don't impress God at all. Don't miss out on Jesus Christ because of the hypocrisy in the church. Take a fresh look at Him in God's Word. The more you see, the more you'll like, because He despises hypocrisy even more than you do.

August 21

Empty Nest

"... so that you do not forget the things which your eyes have seen and they do not depart from your heart all the days of your life; but make them known to your sons and your grandsons."
—Deuteronomy 4:9

Have you ever thought about how parenting is a continual process of letting go? James Dobson says, "Parents must grant their children independence consistent with their age and maturity. When a child can tie his shoes, let him. When he can walk safely to school, let him." This prepares them (and us) to leave the nest, but it isn't always easy to do.

For many Baby Boomers, the empty nest is a constantly emerging reality. To prepare for that time, parents must remember that parenting is learning to let go and using the time we have with our children as a time of preparation for adulthood.

In that light, a verse in Proverbs is a great verse to live by: "Train up a child in the way he should go and when he is old, he will not depart from it." In short, the best way to be ready to let go of our kids is to prepare them to live responsible, godly lives on their own.

August 22

LEADERS ARE COURAGEOUS

"Have I not commanded you? Be strong and courageous!
Do not tremble or be dismayed,
for the LORD your God is with you wherever you go."
—Joshua 1:9

Obviously, leaders make things happen; they bring about change. Leaders also:

- Clearly communicate what they stand for—what their goals are. They have clear direction.
- Have an ability to motivate others to do what they want them to do. People *want* to follow leaders. Sometimes this is for good, sometimes it is for evil.
- Delegate. They trust others to get the job done. They know constant micromanaging destroys the morale of those they are called to lead.

All these are key traits of leadership, but what separates ordinary leaders from *extraordinary* or great leaders?

I believe that it's courage—the courage to do what's right and to do what needs to be done, especially when the heat is on and people are grumbling, and times are hard. Great leaders have the courage to lead others to carry out their vision no matter how hard the course. This courage can be found in the Lord.

Leaders, God's Word says, "Be strong and courageous." Courage is the key in all great leaders.

August 23

THE FIRST MILE

*"... let us run with endurance the race that is set before us,
fixing our eyes on Jesus, the author and perfecter of faith ..."*
—Hebrews 12:1–2

So much is said about going the extra mile, and that's a good thing. Jesus Christ taught us to go the extra mile in serving others. But we often overlook the importance of going the first mile. Joggers know, when in training, it is not always the third or fourth mile that is the toughest, but the first mile! To just get started can sometimes be our biggest challenge.

How do you start your day? You probably have a whole list of things to accomplish. Sometimes there is so much stuff, we are so overwhelmed that we don't know where to start. Other times we jump over some very important things, knowing there are so many other things to do. Start that first mile of the day by quietly spending a few moments in Scripture and prayer and you will find the rest of the day is much easier to navigate.

Remember, whether you are training for the big road race, or simply for the daily race of life, the extra mile does not mean anything unless you faithfully go the first one.

CALLING

". . . for the gifts and the calling of God are irrevocable."
—Romans 11:29

What is a calling? Can anyone get one? Sometimes people struggle to understand what a calling is. It sounds so mysterious.

A calling is an invitation or summons to leave what we're doing to serve someone who needs us. It always involves feelings of inadequacy, because it moves us out of our comfort zone. It always involves sacrifice, unselfishness, and commitment for us to use our talents, abilities, and life experiences to serve God and man. A calling of God is always an inner leading from Him, which is consistent with Scripture.

Can anybody be called?

Everybody is. For the highest calling in life is not to be a teacher or public servant, not to be a pastor or a doctor, but to be a Christian and a follower in faith of Jesus. It's a calling for life and for eternity that you don't want to miss.

Have you accepted life's highest calling?

EMPTINESS

"The conclusion, when all has been heard, is: fear God and keep
His commandments, because this applies to every person."
—Ecclesiastes 12:13

Do you ever feel like you've done it all? Success, wealth, pleasure, thrills, and yet you feel empty inside? Solomon, the ancient king of Israel, was such a man. He had extraordinary success and wealth, incredible intellect, more women and sex than Wilt Chamberlain, and yet it all became meaningless to him. He felt so empty inside because he turned his back on God to pursue what he wanted for himself. He was a classic example of a good man who started strong, but turned wrong, and wound up empty.

A Just Result

"Whatever your hand finds to do, do it with all your might . . ."
—Ecclesiastes 9:10

As a teenager, I went to work in a tennis shop learning to string racquets. The owner told me I'd have to practice on old racquets for a couple of weeks before he'd let me get paid to string customers' racquets. After a few weeks, he gave me a brand new Jack Kramer racquet to string for one of his best customers. In the dark ages of the twentieth century, there were no finer racquets.

I worked carefully and slowly, and when I was finished, I said to the shop owner, "I hope he likes it, because that's the best I can do." He looked it over and smiled and said, "I hope so, too, because it's yours."

That man gave me a gift that lasted long after the racquet gave out. We need to do our best to treat folks like we want to be treated because we never know when our actions may come back to bless us, or haunt us. God's Word is clear, "Whatever a man sows, this he will also reap."

August 27

CHURCH

"How blessed is the one whom You choose and bring near to You to dwell in Your courts. We will be satisfied with the goodness of Your house, Your holy temple."
—Psalm 65:4

How do you feel about church? Do you think it's full of hypocrites? A place for weaklings? A self-righteous religious club?

All those charges may be true. After all, churches are made up of people, and people are not perfect. Imperfect people make for imperfect churches. If you ever find a perfect church, please don't join it. You'll mess it up in a second.

The church is a hospital for sinners, not a hotel for saints. It's a place where people go to improve their spiritual health. It's a place where people go for encouragement, and to get their spiritual batteries recharged.

For non-Christians, it's where they learn what it means to follow Christ and how to have a relationship with God. Why not give church a try? After all, what makes you think you're going to like heaven if you don't want to be with God's people on earth?

A Man after God's Own Heart

". . . I have sinned against the LORD . . ."
—2 Samuel 12:13

Adultery. Murder. Abuse of power. Do these sound like the actions of someone who would have a special place in God's heart?

Surprisingly, the Bible shows us that King David was a man who found special favor with God, even though he was guilty of all those things. But the Bible also shows us that David recognized his mistakes and called them what they were—sins against God. He asked God's forgiveness and committed himself to living God's way.

Even though we may not have done what David did, we have all sinned. God's Word says, "While we were yet sinners, Christ died for us." He died to pay the penalty for our sins and to offer us forgiveness.

When you mess up, confess your sin to God just like David did. Ask for God's forgiveness and for strength to resist sin in the future. Anything you say won't be a surprise to Him. He knows everything. But He is the only answer to man's ultimate problem of sin.

The Schools

"... blessed are they who keep my ways.
Heed instruction and be wise, and do not neglect it."
—Proverbs 8:32–33

The twentieth century was a time of radical change in our education system. A study of the Fullerton, California, school system compared the problems in the 1940's to the 1980's, and the differences were astounding. In the forties, the major problems with students were truancy, running in the halls, talking in class, and chewing gum. In the eighties, the major problems included teenage pregnancy, violence, stealing, rape, bringing knives and guns to school, drug abuse, and vandalism. Now, with shootings in our schools, the problems are even worse.

When we hear results like this, we realize the tremendous decline of values in society. I encourage you to look to the Ten Commandments. The fact is, you can't find better guidance for teaching our children how to live successful lives and how to care for their fellow man than the Big Ten. Why not begin by teaching them to your children? Society will be a better place because of it.

CLEAVE

". . . [he] shall give happiness to his wife whom he has taken."
—Deuteronomy 24:5

When God's Word says of marriage, "A man shall leave his father and mother and *cleave* to his wife," the word, cleave, means to join together, to glue, or to cement. This implies that there will always be pressures on the marriage to pull apart.

Pressures like:

- *Busyness* leaves little quality time.
- *Work* can become all-consuming.
- *Demands of children.* Children are a blessing and we feel so responsible, but our spouse is to come first.
- *Money,* how it's earned, saved, consumed, or wasted. It can become an idol and put before our spouse.
- *Health problems* are the reason wedding vows include "in sickness and in health."
- *Infidelity.* This is the big one, and can be devastating.

Yet when a husband and wife *commit* to cleave, no matter what, and look to God for strength and help, a marriage can withstand any pressure seeking to pull it apart.

August 31

TALENTS

*"For to everyone who has, more shall be given,
and he will have an abundance . . ."*
—Matthew 25:29

A wealthy man who had three servants was going on a long trip. He gave one servant five talents, another two talents, and the other servant one talent. In those days, one talent was a large sum of money, so he told each one to make good use of what he had entrusted to them so he could realize a good increase of his investment when he returned.

The five-talent man doubled his talents to ten. The two-talent man doubled his to four. And the one talent man, fearing he might lose it, refused to take risks or even to try so he just buried his.

When the master returned, he heard the report of the five- and two-talent servants. He gave them equal praise, for they both made the most of what was entrusted to them. But the one-talent man who produced nothing, made him furious and he took the talent and gave it to the servant with ten.

September 1

LONG-TERM CONSEQUENCES OF SIN

"For he who does wrong will receive the consequences of the wrong which he has done . . ."
—**Colossians 3:25**

I'm haunted by the biblical story of Sarah and Abraham, where God promised them a child to build a great nation. They were past the normal childbearing years, but Sarah had an idea. There was a custom in those days that if the husband had a child by his wife's maid, the child could legally be his wife's child. So Sarah said to Abraham, "Sleep with my maid." He was glad to oblige.

The Egyptian maid had a child. Sarah became insanely jealous and eventually ran the maid and her son off. His name was Ishmael, from which many Arabic people are descended. Later, God gave Sarah and Abraham a child. He was named Isaac, and from him would come Israel and the Jewish people.

Because Sarah did not trust God's promise, it led to sibling rivalry between Ishmael and Isaac, a rivalry and animosity that exists to this day in the Middle East between Arabs and Jews.

Sin brings long-term consequences. Let's make it easier on ourselves and others. Let's do things God's way, through faith.

September 2

THE LIGHTHOUSE

"... he who walks in the darkness does not know
where he goes."
—John 12:35

Tom Landry tells the story of a captain of a battleship who, in the middle of the night, saw the light of another ship coming directly at him. The captain radioed the oncoming ship and said, "Turn south immediately."

The response was, "You turn south immediately."

The captain was furious. He radioed back, "This is a battleship. I command you to turn south immediately."

The response was, "This is the lighthouse. You turn south immediately."

Often we have an attitude like that captain's. We are arrogant toward God and mankind. We expect others to get out of our way, and we ignore God's guidance for living life. Then suddenly we find ourselves shipwrecked and feeling like fools.

Jesus Christ is the lighthouse trying to warn us of danger and lead us to safety. I encourage you to trust Christ and be willing to follow His leadership in your life. He will keep you out of a lot of trouble.

September 3

HOW TO HATE EVIL AND BE A LOVING PERSON

"Abhor what is evil; cling to what is good."
—**Romans 12:9**

How can you hate evil and be a loving person? It sure isn't easy in today's world. So often the world teaches that what is evil is good, and what is good is evil. But the Bible says, "Abhor what is evil and cling to what is good." Can you do this and be a loving person?

Do you even know what evil is?

Let me suggest this: Jesus is the perfect picture of God in a man. What He says is evil . . . is evil. What He says is good . . . is good. No one has ever hated evil more than Jesus, and no one has ever been more loving than Jesus. His life, His spirit, and His character show us how to hate evil while being a truly loving person. Hate what Jesus hates . . . sin. And love those Jesus loves . . . people, all people. This will get you off to a good start in hating evil and being a loving person.

Self-Control

"But [a] fruit of the Spirit . . . is self-control."
—Galatians 5:22–23

Do you ever say, "It was just too tempting," or "I wish I hadn't lost my cool?"

A key to successful living is self-control: controlling our emotions, desires, passions, or tongue. Self-control is about self-discipline. The Bible compares it to sports. It says, "Run your race to win. Everyone who competes in the games exercises self-control in all things." Self-control is essential to success in living, as well as in sports.

Let me suggest a few ways to learn it:

1. Clarify your purpose. What are you trying to accomplish? Is it to lose a few pounds? Your decisions will be shaped by your purpose.
2. Be honest with yourself about where you lack self-control. Alcoholics who find victory over booze know the first step is admitting their inability to control the problem.
3. Ask God for self-discipline, and
4. Take action on that discipline one day at a time. Self-control is a real key to successful living.

September 5

Spiritual Sissies or Spiritual Men

*"For I have chosen him, so that he may command his children
and his household after him to keep the way of the LORD
by doing righteousness and justice . . ."*
—Genesis 18:19

So many men today are real spiritual sissies. Not spiritual men, but spiritual wimps. Men, if you're not interested in being a real man, the kind of leader in the home that God is calling you to be, this is not a message for you. Go on being gutless wonders just like so many men are when it comes to spiritual leadership in the home. But if you're interested in being a *real* man, realize God has called you to lead.

Jesus Christ tells us we're to be servant leaders—not dictatorial leaders—but servant leaders, like He *was* with His church, and *is* with His church today. He gave His life for us. Men, wake up. Our families need us. Our nation needs us to be real men—spiritual leaders in the home. And, remember, you lead your family by allowing Christ to lead you.

September 6

REAL LOVE IS

"[Love] bears all things, believes all things,
hopes all things, endures all things."
—1 Corinthians 13:7

What is real love? Love is not lust or emotion or sentimentalism. It's not tolerance, which often translates into intolerance of godliness and apathy toward evil. What is love?

The Bible tells us the highest love is not based on feelings, but is a commitment of our will. It is given unconditionally to another person, no matter how they respond. The Bible tells us this love is patient and kind. It's not envious, arrogant, or rude. It's not selfish or easily angered. It's not like a resentment accountant who keeps a record of how others have wronged us. Love hates evil and rejoices in the truth. Real love puts up with a lot, and endures it with hope.

The Bible tells us God is love. He shows us this real love perfectly in Jesus, Who truly loves you. Yes, Jesus loves you. Have faith in Him and you'll experience the greatest love you've ever known.

September 7

Marriage and Divorce

"... What therefore God has joined together,
let no man separate."
—Matthew 19:6

An understandable argument for same-sex marriage is that the high rate of divorce has done more to harm the family than same-sex marriage ever would. It's a legitimate point that exposes obvious hypocrisy in the church today.

Jesus was once asked, "Is it ever lawful for a man to divorce his wife for any reason at all?" Jesus answered the question about divorce by talking about marriage. He said, "He who created them from the beginning made them male and female. For this reason a man shall leave his father and mother and be joined to his wife and the two shall become one flesh . . . what therefore God has joined together, let no man separate."

In short, God's intention for marriage is "only between a man and a woman, for life." This speaks to the need for repentance in the church when it comes to marriage commitment. Jesus upheld God's original plan for marriage, and so should we.

September 8

RESPECTING OUR PARENTS

"Every one of you shall reverence his mother and his father . . ."
—Leviticus 19:3

The Bible commands us to honor our parents. This command has three major phases starting with Phase 1—obeying when we are children, and ending with Phase 3—caring for our parents' needs when they're unable to care for themselves. Phase 2, the middle phase, is usually the longest. It's that time when we become adult children and our parents can still meet their own needs. In this phase, we are called to respect our parents.

Respect doesn't mean obedience. Parents of adult children need to remember this, just as adult children need to remember it. Respect means seeking their input when appropriate, yet most of all, doing what God wants you to do. Respect means showing them love and spending time with them.

To the parents of adult children: are you helping, or hindering, the opportunity for respect? You may be pushing your adult child away. Remember, respect breeds respect.

The middle phase of honoring our parents is the longest. Let's make the most of it . . . both parent *and* child.

Just Do It

"Abide in Me, and I in you. As the branch cannot
bear fruit of itself unless it abides in the vine,
so neither can you unless you abide in Me."
—John 15:4

Everyone has seen a Nike commercial. The implication is that all that's needed to become an athlete is determination, hard work, and those shoes. When it comes to human nature, life is very different. Human beings just aren't disciplined enough to do all we need to do. We can't change ourselves by our own initiative.

One of the Bible writers, an avid sports fan by the name of Paul, recognized that changing human nature calls for something else—a supernatural change agent. Our only responsibility is to be willing to allow that change agent to bring about the needed improvements.

No, He might not improve your golf game, even though you wish He would. He may not give you the ability to hit home runs. But He will adjust your attitude, your character, and your relationships for the better. So, *just do it*. Allow Christ to change you from an ineffective, frustrated self-improver, into a winner in the game of life.

September 10

GRANDPARENTS— A KEY RELATIONSHIP

"Grandchildren are the crown of old men . . ."
—Proverbs 17:6

Isn't it amazing how the normal conflicts in the parent-child relationship don't seem to be a problem with grandparents and grandchildren? Grandparents may have old-fashioned values, but they're admired by their grandchildren.

What do you think of when you think of a beloved grandparent? Even hardened cynics often get misty-eyed when recalling memories of a grandparent, yet grandparents are often the forgotten victims of divorce and separation. In June of 2000, the Supreme Court defended the parents' right to restrict or cut off ties with the grandparents of their children.

Parents, let's do all we can to enhance the relationship between our children and their grandparents. It's part of their heritage that they need to understand. It's part of their identity that makes them whole. God's Word says, "Grandchildren are the crown of old men." If at all possible, don't deny them their crown.

September 11

ONE QUESTION FOR GOD

". . . do not lead us into temptation, but deliver us from evil."
—Matthew 6:13

George Barna polled Americans: "If you could ask God one question, what would it be?" The number one answer was, "Why is there so much pain and suffering?"

In light of September 11, 2001, follow-up thoughts are raised. If God is all-powerful and all-knowing, yet doesn't stop evil, why should I believe in Him? Or, if He can't do anything about it, He isn't much of a God, is He?

Two things to keep in mind: God gets blamed for a lot of man's evil, but God has given man a free will. Ironically, the more victimized people are by man's evil, the more they tend to blame God. But we are not created as computers, programmed to do good or evil. Like God, we can make choices.

Why does God, who is all-loving and all-powerful, allow suffering and evil? No answer is adequate, but God's main concern is that we trust Him to bring good out of evil. If He did it when mankind murdered His innocent Son, He can do it with September 11, 2001.

Religion Causes More Wars

*"Pure and undefiled religion in the sight of our God and Father
is this . . . to keep oneself unstained by the world."*
—James 1:27

Another major objection to Christianity is, "Religion is the cause of more problems and wars than anything else." The response? You're right. Religion *is* the cause of many wars and conflicts:

- Look at the Middle East today.
- Consider the abuses in church history.
- The Crusades were the so-called Christian holy wars with Moslems seeking to capture the Holy Land for the "true faith."
- There was the horror of the Inquisition, with so-called heretics burned at the stake, and Jews expelled from Spain.
- Remember the terror and killing in Northern Ireland, or more recently, look at September 11, 2001 . . . hate smothered with perverted religion.

Jesus never taught this. He says to love and forgive your enemies. There has been some bad stuff in religion, but Jesus would never call on Christians to force other people to believe in Him and His Word. Nothing in the Bible teaches that. That is manmade religion—not Jesus. Yes, a lot of religion stinks. It has caused tons of unnecessary problems. But Jesus is the One you want to look to. Unlike misguided religion, what He teaches is always good.

September 13

WHEN PRAYER DISAPPOINTS

"You ask and do not receive,
because you ask with wrong motives . . ."
—James 4:3

You'll find little argument from people about the importance of prayer. Most people pray. Everyone needs it. But the reality is, prayer is often disappointing. We don't get the results we desire. Let me share with you why: It's found in the Bible, in the book of James. "You ask and do not receive because you ask selfishly."

Prayer is not so much asking God for what *we* want, it's finding out what *He* wants, and finding the strength to do it. Selfish prayers disappoint. Prayers to get to know God, to find strength and to do His will, bring tremendous results—sometimes supernatural results. This kind of praying is powerful, because you get plugged in to the ultimate power source—the God of the universe.

How's your prayer life? Fulfilling, or disappointing? Remember your motive, for your heart is the key. Why don't you take a moment right now and talk with God for the expressed purpose of seeking His will? You'll be pleased with the results!

September 14

Extra Mile Service

"Whoever forces you to go one mile, go with him two."
—**Matthew 5:41**

My wife and I were staying in a nice hotel for a special occasion. One day we went to the pool, and before we could get seated attendants brought us towels and ice water. After I went jogging, a bellman gave me a bottle of water as I entered the lobby. They kept surprising us with unexpected, extra-mile service.

I really believe that any corporation, organization, or ministry where extra mile service is a part of the culture will have a greater impact for good. Extra-mile service goes beyond what is expected.

Do you know who originated the idea? Jesus Christ. He said, "Whoever forces you to go one mile, go with him two." Rome ruled their culture, and it was legal for Roman soldiers to ask a civilian to help them carry their armor for one mile, at any time. The people greatly resented it. What Jesus taught was shocking. But following Jesus calls for extra-mile service. Even if you don't follow Him, that service is always appreciated.

Pseudo Grief

"... THEY ALWAYS GO ASTRAY IN THEIR HEART,
AND THEY DID NOT KNOW MY WAYS...."
—Hebrews 3:10

A modern day phenomenon in the age of TV is the irrational out-pouring of pseudo grief. People grieve more intensely for an image they've never personally known than they do for a neighbor or family member.

We saw this most dramatically with the deaths of Lady Di and JFK. Both represented what society saw as the best of their nation's royalty. Both were young, glamorous, attractive, and wealthy. They were the ideal in the world's eyes. Yet, most of us didn't know them. We just knew the image on the screen.

Do you care more for images than the real people in your life?

Whom do you grieve for the most when they're gone? If it's an image on TV, you're living a pseudo life—not a real life. Real living comes with real relationships and, sometimes, with loss that involves real grief. But when that loss comes, a real relationship with God will get you through that grief. Real relationships have real pain, but they also have real meaning. Meaningful relationships with God and your fellow man are essential to real living.

September 16

ENVIRONMENTAL CONCERN

"... God said to them ... 'Rule over the fish of the sea
and over the birds of the sky and over every living thing
that moves on the earth.'"
—Genesis 1:28

There's a great deal of concern about the environment these days. That's good, for the very first chapter of the Bible, Genesis 1, tells us that one of man's major responsibilities is to care for the environment. You could say Genesis 1 is the ultimate environmental manifesto.

With this environmental concern comes tremendous confusion, and it lies with the wrong focus. Some environmentalists worship nature more than the God of all nature. Some worship creation more than the Creator. It is as ludicrous as having a greater awe for the painting, Mona Lisa, than for her creator, Leonardo da Vinci.

When nature is supreme, we get confused and misguided. When nature is respected and managed out of obedience to God, the Creator, we are able to care for the environment in a way that makes sense; a way that's best for all.

September 17

BLAME GAME

"A fool does not delight in understanding,
but only in revealing his own mind."
—Proverbs 18:2

Often, spouses blame their mates for their problems. One woman finally had enough. She went to her lawyer, saying her husband was driving her crazy. She wanted a divorce.

The lawyer asked, "Do you have any grounds?"

She said, "Yes, we have four or five acres."

The lawyer thought this might be interesting. He then asked, "Does he beat you up?"

She responded, "No, I get up before that bum every morning."

The lawyer dropped his pen and said, "Well, why do you want a divorce?"

She replied, "My idiot husband can't carry on an intelligent conversation."

The blame game always makes us look foolish in the end. If you are struggling in your marriage:

- Ask God for help and forgiveness where you have fallen short.
- Ask God to help you forgive your spouse.
- Ask your spouse to forgive where you have fallen short.
- Love, respect, and affirm your spouse daily.

You may be surprised that your spouse ain't so bad after all; moreover, they may very well feel the same.

September 18

MID-LIFE BLUES

"Whatever you do in word or deed,
do all in the name of the Lord Jesus,
giving thanks through Him to God the Father."
—Colossians 3:17

Mid-life has come, and is about to go, for the Baby Boomers! The thought of millions of boomers in a mid-life crisis can unsettle even the most stable mind. Mid-life is the time when hard-driving adults begin to grow weary of all their responsibilities. They can feel trapped. Boredom may kick in as they realize their goals. Depression may set in from goals that have not been realized and never will be.

Bob Buford calls this stage of life halftime. In sports, halftime is when the teams regroup, catch their breath, go out and do better in the second half. Buford says the key to getting through a mid-life crisis is shifting focus from success to significance.

I propose that the key to lasting significance lies in meaningful relationships—relationships with God, family, and friends. It's found in doing your best with the gifts and talents God has given you. It's found in living life God's way.

Mid-life is a key time to get those things right, before the second half begins. If you're at mid-life, seek to shift your focus from success to significance. If you do, your second half can be even better than your first.

September 19

REAPING WHAT YOU SOW

"Do not be deceived, God is not mocked;
for whatever a man sows, this he will also reap."
—Galatians 6:7

A young teenager wanted to aggravate the hard-working farmer who lived next door. He and some of his pals sneaked into the farmer's field one night and spread crabgrass seeds all over the farm. Soon, the crabgrass came up. He laughed every time he saw the farmer vainly trying to get rid of it.

A few years later, long after the teenager forgot his prank, he fell in love with the farmer's daughter and they were married. When her father died he inherited the farm and for the rest of his life he battled that sorry crabgrass he had spread all over the fields.

The Bible says, "For whatever a man sows, this he will also reap." In short, when we're hard on others, they tend to be hard on us. It's the law of the harvest. When you plant tomatoes, you don't get squash, for the harvest never lies.

What kind of seeds are you sowing and what kind of harvest are you reaping? Let's remember—in life, we reap what we sow.

September 20

HUSBANDS, UNDERSTAND YOUR WIVES NEED SECURITY

"You husbands . . .
live with your wives in an understanding way."
—1 Peter 3:7

Part of husbands loving their wives is showing understanding toward them. God's Word says, "Husbands, live with your wives in an understanding way." Part of understanding is knowing her need for romance. But another part of understanding your wife is meeting her need for security. God's Word says we are to remember she is the weaker vessel.

Now ladies, before you start screaming, realize that this does not mean women are weaker than men intellectually, spiritually, emotionally, or relationally. Often, women are stronger than men relationally, but they are usually weaker physically. In a world where some men may not have the best intentions toward women, women can feel vulnerable, and in need of protection. Providing security for your wife is a way of letting her know you love her. It meets a great need she hopes you'll fulfill.

September 21

PRESSURE

"... having shod YOUR FEET WITH THE PREPARATION OF
THE GOSPEL OF PEACE ... "
—Ephesians 6:15

People live pressure-filled lives and it's taking its toll. Dr. Joel Elkes says, "Our mode of life—the way we live—is emerging as today's main cause of illness." The American Academy of Family Physicians says that two-thirds of all visits to doctors are stress related, and that stress is now known as the major contributor to heart disease, cancer, accidental injuries, and suicide.

People attend stress seminars and devour books on stress. Sometimes they find that just focusing on it makes them more uptight. But, let's face it. Stress and pressure are a part of life.

Even Jesus Christ promised us that we'll all face it. He said, "In this world you'll face much tribulation." Tribulation also means pressure. He goes on to say, "but take heart. I have overcome the world." Jesus does not promise us freedom from pressure, but He does promise us peace in the midst of the stress. Inner peace is a by-product of knowing Christ as Savior and Lord. The good news? It's available to all who trust in Him.

Yes, pressure is a part of life, but Christ gives us peace amidst the pressure. And that's not a bad way to live!

September 22

KNOWING THE TRUTH

"And the Word became flesh, and dwelt among us,
and we saw His glory . . . full of grace and truth."
—John 1:14

To know Jesus we need to know Scripture, for Jesus teaches, "Thy Word is truth." Do you believe this?

Today, very few believe in absolute truth, yet Scripture records that Jesus said He is the truth. Jesus claims to be absolute truth. Truth is found in a person, not a religion, not a philosophy, and not a code of morality. The absolute truth about God is found in Jesus. And the truth of Jesus is discovered in Scripture. Thus, Jesus and Scripture are not mutually exclusive.

We cannot know truth unless we know Jesus. We cannot know Jesus unless we know Scripture. Therefore, we have to decide if what Jesus says about Scripture is true. Are Jesus and the Word absolute truth? Absolutely! God reveals Himself in a person, and God reveals that person in His Word, for Jesus says, "Thy word is truth."

September 23

THE CHECKBOOK DOESN'T LIE

*"Now this I say, he who sows sparingly will also reap sparingly,
and he who sows bountifully will also reap bountifully."*
—2 Corinthians 9:6

I had an interesting conversation with a friend who is an atheist. He had visited our church and heard statistics on the high number of families who give nothing to the Lord's work each year. The basic minimum in faithful giving, according to the Bible, is ten percent, or a tithe. My friend said to me, "I was shocked. I thought if you people really believe this stuff about God, heaven, and hell, and the importance of spreading the message, you'd want to give *more* than ten percent. What could be more important than that?"

Jesus would agree, for He clearly said, "Where your treasure is, there your heart will be." In short, where you spend your money reveals the priorities of your heart. What does your checkbook say about your priorities? The checkbook doesn't lie. To all you who profess to be Christians, what does your checkbook say about your faith in God? Do you really believe what you profess to believe?

September 24

THE VARSITY DRIVE-IN

". . . yet not My will, but Yours be done."
—Luke 22:42

"What'll ya have? What'll ya have? What'll ya have?"
If you are from the Atlanta area, these familiar words exemplify quick service for tasty food from a restaurant named *The Varsity* which is steeped in tradition. Many people feel that prayer is like putting in an order for what we want. Yet prayer is, most of all, about getting to know God and His will for our lives. One of the ways God teaches us His will is by not always giving us what we want. You say, "What's wrong with getting what I want?" Nothing, if it's God's best. But if it's not, there are always negative consequences, so be careful what you ask for!

Prayer is powerful in allowing us to connect with God, but it's not at all about God simply saying, "What'll ya have?" It's about discovering what He wants for our lives.

Perhaps the question should be reversed to "Lord, what'll Ya have of *me?*"

Nothing Is Impossible with God

"... Jesus said, 'With people it is impossible, but not with God;
for all things are possible with God.'"
—Mark 10:27

One of the greatest verses in the Bible is, "For nothing will be impossible with God." Do you believe it? It's what the angel told Mary, the mother of Jesus, when he announced she would give birth as a virgin to God's son.

If you are facing a particularly tough challenge where you need strength and wisdom beyond yourself, will you believe nothing will be impossible with God? If you are in a season of grief, and not sure you can make it, will you believe nothing will be impossible with God? If you are facing discouragement, disappointment, depression, or despair, will you believe nothing will be impossible with God? If you are struggling in your family, will you believe nothing is impossible with God? Mary did, and because she did, Jesus came to be our Savior. He died and rose, conquering sin and death for you and me. The story of Jesus reminds us that nothing is impossible with God.

September 26

A Great Prayer
for Your Children

"For this reason also . . . we have not ceased to pray for you . . ."
—Colossians 1:9

We need to pray for our children. For many years my wife has prayed a prayer from Scripture for our three sons. Here are some ideas to try:

- *Pray that they will increase in the knowledge of God.* Most parents' greatest hope for their children is that they will be happy, but a fulfilled life comes from knowing God. Without God, there is a nagging emptiness. Lots of people know *about* God, but knowing Him personally is different. We all know a lot *about* our nation's president but only a few know him personally.
- *Pray that they live a worthy life.* Pray that their lives will have an impact for good, and that they will be people of trustworthy character.
- *Pray that they're strengthened in God's power.* The world and evil influences will seek to pull our children down. They need God's power to be strong, to resist temptation, and to do the right thing.
- *And, thank God for each child.* They are unique creations of God.

We all need to pray for our children. I hope these thoughts help.

WHAT IS YOUR ULTIMATE AUTHORITY FOR MAKING DECISIONS?

"All Scripture is inspired by God and profitable for teaching, for reproof, for correction, for training in righteousness."
—2 Timothy 3:16

What is your ultimate authority for making important decisions? Is it your knowledge? Intuition? Your experience? Is it people you want to please? Is it contemporary culture? Is it a synagogue, church, or certain spiritual leader?

I want to suggest God's Word. God has created you for a purpose. He knows how you work best. The way He speaks through His written Word, and it is perfectly true. It applies to every age, race, and nation.

The Bible is clear on some things like murder, stealing, adultery, and forgiveness. When it doesn't speak to a specific issue—like which mutual funds to invest in, whom to marry, or stem cell research, it gives perfect principles we need to know in order to make the best decisions —those that are pleasing to God.

So try reading it. Start with the New Testament. Ask God to speak to you through His Word. When it comes to living well, God's Word knows best.

PORN

"... do not give the devil an opportunity."
—Ephesians 4:27

Porn has invaded the home through the Internet. And now the worst, most hardcore pornography is available to any child, teen, or adult who can click on a computer or a dial a cell phone.

A poll by the Kaiser Family Foundation found that seventy percent of 15 to 17 year olds accidentally come across porn online. Internet pornography has been called the crack cocaine of sexual addiction. It's often justified in the name of freedom, but it's insidiously evil. It's exploitation of women. It ruins marriages. It puts a man's mind in the gutter. Men will always struggle with lust, and porn is like throwing gasoline on the fire.

Men, put that computer where your wife can always see it. Parents, be sure your computers have blocks and are placed in open areas where they can be monitored.

Those who battle addiction to porn, admit your problem to God. Ask His help and get some help. You'll be a real man if you do.

VICTORY OVER

"No temptation has overtaken you but such as is common to man; and God is faithful, who will not allow you to be tempted beyond what you are able, but with the temptation will provide the way of escape also, so that you will be able to endure it."
—1 Corinthians 10:13

Let's talk about temptation. How do you keep a decision to do wrong from getting the best of you?

Realize that temptation is a part of life. The Bible tells us Jesus was tempted in *every* way we are. The big difference between Jesus and all of us is that He never gave in to it.

How can we keep temptation from getting the best of us?

- *Just say no.* Don't take time to flirt with it, or even argue. Just say no.
- *Ask God's help to resist it.* For things too tough to resist, things you battle constantly, simply admit they're too tough and ask God's help in resisting them. The power used by the only Man to never give in to temptation is available to all of us. We just need to confess our weakness and admit our need for Him and His strength.
- Then *scram.* Get out of there! This is one time in life when running is not cowardly, but the bravest thing you can do.

September 30

FOOTBALL

"In that day His feet will stand on the Mount of Olives,
which is in front of Jerusalem on the east . . ."
—Zechariah 14:4

I love football season—fans cheering, the big games, the great rivalries. With every new season there's always anticipation and hope. Will the players rise to the challenge, or will some bad play cost the team a game, or even a season? And, certainly, no play in football is more important than the touchdown—the goal of every drive.

Did you know, the Bible speaks about a touchdown, the greatest touchdown ever? It's something Jews and Christians alike will agree on. The Bible says it's going to happen just as time is running out, at the end of the game. The Messiah is going to touch down on the Mount of Olives in Israel. The Scriptures teach us the great touchdown will occur by a man named Jesus.

He's coming for those who are on His team, and to judge those who are not. His touchdown will mean victory for His team, and lasting defeat for the opponents. The question is . . . are you going to be one who celebrates His touchdown, or one who loses the ultimate game of life?

October 1

WOE TO YOU CHURCH HYPOCRITES

"Let your light shine before men in such a way that they may see your good works, and glorify your Father who is in heaven."
—Matthew 5:16

George Barna, in an article entitled *U.S. Christians' Influence Invisible,* states: "Christians don't impact America because their lives don't reflect their beliefs . . . and they aren't sufficiently different from the people around them to make a difference in the lives of non-believers."

For more than a decade, studies have consistently shown that Christianity seems to be losing its influence in people's lives. Rather than shaping the way a person lives, it seems to have little effect at all. Ironically, this occurs at the same time Americans are much more interested in spiritual things.

Hey Christians, wake up! Don't you realize the more our character and spirit reflect Jesus, the more people see Him and are drawn to Him?

Is your life more a reflection of the culture around you than the spirit and character of Jesus Christ? What would your neighbors say? Your co-workers? Your family? It's something to think about.

October 2

FORGIVENESS

". . . pardon, and you will be pardoned."
—Luke 6:37

Do you sometimes struggle with feelings of bitterness and resentment? Perhaps when a person at work gets a promotion you feel you deserved, or when a friend or spouse betrays you, feelings of bitterness and resentment creep in.

Let me tell you about a person who had every reason to be bitter. He was accused of being a troublemaker, and He only told the truth. One of His closest aides betrayed Him and turned Him in to the authorities. At His trial, people made up lies about Him. He was beaten by the guards. He was sentenced to death by a judge responding to a lynch mob. While He was being executed and people were making fun of Him, He prayed, "Father, forgive them, for they don't know what they're doing."

I'm talking about Jesus Christ, the person who had every reason to feel bitter, but chose to forgive. Let Jesus Christ be your model to follow. Ask God to help you forgive the person who wronged you, and you'll feel free at last.

October 3

OPRAH

". . . [they] will turn away their ears from the truth
and will turn aside to myths."
—2 Timothy 4:4

There's a good possibility that the most influential spiritual leader in America today is Oprah Winfrey. Her spirituality is an eclectic smorgasbord of religious and spiritual ideas. She's overwhelmingly for universalism. Universalists believe that everyone gets to God their own way—no one religion has exclusive rights on heaven. It's the dominant theological idea inside and outside the American church. And Oprah is its most winsome and popular proponent.

It makes me wonder how she would react if Jesus Christ was her featured guest. How would she respond to His outrageous claim, "I am the way, the truth, the life. No one comes to the Father except through Me"?

Would she say, "Jesus, there are lots of ways to heaven."

Or would she say, "Oh, my goodness, forgive me. I've been leading millions down the wrong path."

It would be an interesting interview—because Jesus' way to heaven and Oprah's way are exact opposites. Who do you think is right?

I'll go with Jesus.

October 4

Marriage and the Future

"You shall not do at all what we are doing here today, every man doing whatever is right in his own eyes . . ."
—Deuteronomy 12:8

Consider the logical result of same-sex marriage. If modern man suddenly decrees that what has been immoral and illegal for thousands of years in every society is now moral and legal, how can he deny a man the right to marry two, three, or four wives—especially since Islam's Koran teaches this as OK.

If same-sex marriage is right and good after being wrong for thousands of years, how can society deny the right for two consenting adults who want to be married—even though they may be father and daughter, mother and son, or brother and sister? On what basis could society say this is wrong, but same-sex marriage is OK? Same-sex marriage ushers in a multitude of legal quagmires that will result in moral chaos.

Let me suggest something outrageous. Let's trust God, who originated marriage as a lifetime commitment between a man and a woman. That's still, after all these years, the best way to go.

October 5

A Fountain Pen

"For as he thinks within himself, so he is."
—Proverbs 23:7

Have you heard that the fountain pen is making a comeback? After many years of neglect, fountain pens are once again in vogue. Made of fine materials and carrying a high price tag, they are now part of the well-dressed, executive look.

There is something interesting about fountain pens. They may look great, but unless they're full of ink, they're really not very useful. Without the right things on the inside, the outside is useless.

The same is true of people. We spend money and time to make the outside attractive. Looking good outside may impress people, but unless there's something inside equally attractive, the outside is merely a covering for ugliness. Only God knows what is inside us. He looks at our heart and our spirit. What does He see in you? Is it ugly, or is it good? The good news is, He offers us a gift, His Son, who will make us beautiful from the inside out. Outward appearance is important, but unless there is something good inside, it's merely a covering for ugliness.

To Be More Like Jesus

*"For all who are being led by the Spirit of God,
these are sons of God."*
—Romans 8:14

There's a lot of talk these days about core values, those distinctives that identify priorities for your company, your family, or your life. Let me share with you the number one core value in our church: *to be more and more like Jesus.*

Think about it. Jesus poured His life into the lives of twelve ordinary men, investing most of His time with them. At one point, He even washed their feet—the act of a slave or a servant. He healed the sick. He loved the poor. He was concerned about the widow, the orphan, and the person left out. He loved kids. He got angry when the religious leaders put the legalism of the Law before the love of God and the love for people. Even when mankind was murdering Him on the cross, He chose to forgive.

Jesus was totally dedicated to doing the will of God, yet He was loving and compassionate and forgiving. Do you have that kind of balance in your life? We all fall short, but what a model to follow in everyday living.

The number one core value at our church is to be like Jesus in spirit and character. What's yours?

October 7

BLIND FROM BIRTH

". . . by what a man is overcome, by this he is enslaved."
—2 Peter 2:19

When I read the story in the New York Times, I couldn't believe it—a blind receiver in football?

He played for Wolford College during the 2002 season. He said he ran his patterns carefully and looked for a dark fuzzy spot coming toward him. Talk about overcoming adversity—this is amazing!

In an age of self-indulgence and a victimization mindset, this player stands out as an example of hard work and perseverance. He has accepted and overcome his adversity, and uses it as a motivation rather than an excuse. By doing so, this young man challenges each of us to not be defeated by our limitations.

Wouldn't all of our lives be more fulfilled and effective if we followed his example? It can happen with God's help. With God as our strength, we won't see ourselves as victims, but as overcomers. Jesus Christ says, "In this world you'll have problems, but take heart. I have overcome the world."

October 8

REAL FAITH AND RAPPELLING

"The faith which you have,
have as your own conviction before God."
—Romans 14:22

There are a lot of definitions of faith. What is *real* faith in God? Some would say it is believing what the Bible says about God, but that's just partial faith. You can believe everything the Bible says is true and not have real faith. How?

Last year my son took me rappelling. I don't like open air heights, but he set the ropes, put me in the harness, said he'd hold the ropes from the ground, and I just needed to jump off a seventy-foot cliff backwards and everything would be fine. Did I believe the ropes were strong enough to hold me? Yes. Did that mean I had real faith? No. It wasn't until I jumped, and entrusted my life to the sureness of the ropes and the dependability of my son that I had faith. *That's* real faith.

We can believe everything in God's Word is true, but until we completely entrust our life and hope for salvation into the hands of Jesus Christ, it's not a real, saving faith.

THE TOUCHDOWN

*"... This Jesus, who has been taken up from you into heaven,
will come in just the same way
as you have watched Him go into heaven."*
—Acts 1:11

In most sports, there is one feat that galvanizes the fans. In golf, it's a hole in one. In basketball, it's the slam-dunk. In baseball, the home run. But in football, it's the touchdown. It always brings fans to their feet.

The objective is simple: The team with the most points wins, and that usually means the most touchdowns. But the greatest and most exciting touchdown has yet to occur, and when it does, the players on the winning team will go wild with joy. Those on the losing team will be devastated in defeat.

The Bible tells about it in the Old and New Testaments. The Messiah will touch down on the Mount of Olives outside Jerusalem when Jesus returns.

Do you believe it? Will you be ready for the ultimate feat?

How you respond in faith to Christ determines whether you are on the winning team, or losing team—forever.

It is my hope you'll be able to celebrate the touchdown when Jesus comes!

October 10

Symphony

*"For You are my rock and my fortress . . .
You will lead me and guide me."*
—Psalm 31:3

What is the most important position in a symphony orchestra? Some would say it's the violins, because they often carry the melody. Others would argue for their favorite instrument. The fact is that the conductor has the most important role of all. Without him, the players would easily go their own way and disharmony and chaos would result. A master conductor leads the symphony to make great music. Without a good conductor, there is no music—only noise.

I have good news for you when it comes to living life successfully. God has provided a Master Conductor. His name is Jesus Christ. When you submit in faith to His leadership, He provides perfect direction and guidance for your life. He shows you how to work well with other people.

Why not allow the Master Conductor to guide your life? Instead of discord and disharmony, He'll help you hit the right notes every single time!

October 11

Is There Other Life in the Universe?

"Lift up your eyes on high and see who has created these stars,
the One who leads forth their host by number . . . the Everlasting
God, the LORD, the Creator of the ends of the earth . . ."
—Isaiah 40:26,28

America's spaceship on Mars produced magnificent views of the Martian landscape. Scientists see unlimited potential for space exploration, and their excitement is contagious. There's so much more to know and explore!

Could there be life on other planets? How do these discoveries affect our view of God? Do we need to revise our understanding of Him?

The answer depends on how big your concept of God is. We need to recognize that God is all mighty, far greater than anything the human mind can conceive. The discoveries of science excite us, but it's even more exciting when we recognize the greatness of the Creator of it all. God is limitless. His creative genius surpasses man's ability to comprehend.

We don't need to fear science or what's out there in space, for in the end, science simply explains to us the creative genius of God. God is over all!

October 12

Earth Pains

"For we know that the whole creation groans
and suffers the pains of childbirth together until now."
—Romans 8:22

Things just ain't what they're supposed to be. Consider man's violence against man, the animal kingdom's survival of the fittest, or pollution poisoning our air and streams. It's incredible how the earth, with all its beauty and wonder, can become a destructive force against itself through earthquakes, volcanoes, hurricanes, and floods.

The Bible says, ". . . the whole creation groans and suffers the pain of childbirth." In the beginning, before man sinned, everything was in sync. There was such peace on earth that man and animals were vegetarians. There was no killing of any kind. But now the earth is in a period that God likens to a mother giving birth; and, like childbirth, things will get worse before they get better.

All creation longs for things to be made right, and one day it will be—the day when Jesus returns. It will be a time of salvation, and judgment. Judgment will be for those who are not right with God, and salvation for those who are. His arrival will usher in a new age of harmony and peace on earth. Won't it be great? If you're ready, yes. If you're not, no. The key question: will you be ready? The only way to be ready is through faith in Jesus Christ.

October 13

THE TRINITY

*". . . great is the mystery of godliness: He who was revealed
in the flesh, was vindicated in the Spirit . . ."*
—1 Timothy 3:16

The Trinity is a theological term to describe God as three persons in one. The actual term is never mentioned in the Bible, but the concept is in the Old and the New Testament.

In the first chapter of the Bible, God says, "Let *Us* make man in *Our* image."

Who do you think us and our are? There is no indication of God being married, so it's not His wife. And angels don't create, they're creations of God. There's only one logical answer: It's God the Father, Son, and Holy Spirit.

When Jesus the Son was baptized, God's Word tells us God the Father spoke from heaven and said, "This is My Son. I'm proud of Him." Then God the Holy Spirit descended upon Him in the form of a dove. All three were there. All three are one God.

It's a mystery our finite human minds have a hard time grasping. But the Trinity—God as three-in-one—fills us with wonder at the unexplainable greatness of God.

October 14

INVOLVED VS. COMMITTED

". . . they first gave themselves to the Lord and to us
by the will of God."
—2 Corinthians 8:5

I love what Lou Holtz, a former South Carolina football coach, has said about his team at the beginning of many seasons. He says they reminded him of the Kamikaze pilot who flew fifty missions—involved, but not committed. He says a lot of players get involved, but time would tell if they were really committed to the cause for the good of the team and committed to helping the team be a success.

On a team, in the office, or in the church, we have a lot of folks who are involved, but not enough are committed to get the job done, no matter what it takes. How about you, when it comes to your life and your responsibilities. Are you just involved, or are you committed to do your best for the good of the team, the group, and all concerned? Most of all, are you committed to do your best for the glory of God, to please Him before anyone else? That's always the key to ultimate success.

October 15

GETTING ALONG WITH THE BOSS

*"Urge bondslaves to be subject to their own masters
in everything, to be well-pleasing, not argumentative . . ."*
—**Titus 2:9**

Most people have a supervisor or a boss. What principles from God's Word can help us get along with our boss?

Submit to his leadership. He or she is the boss. The only time you shouldn't submit is when the boss urges you to do something immoral or dishonest. Then, if you want to please God, you'll do what's right and be willing to face any consequences.

Work heartily to please God. If the goal is to please God, any honorable work is meaningful. Work to please God, and usually the boss is pleased. Every boss is looking for honest, hard-working employees.

Recognize it's not your job to change your boss, but you can always change bosses. If the boss is immoral or unreasonable, you can find a new boss, or become your own boss. This takes guts and faith but it's a blessing of a free country. Seek to get along with your boss God's way, and if you can't, find a new one.

October 16

How To Be a Good Boss

"Masters, grant to your slaves justice and fairness,
knowing that you too have a Master in heaven."
—**Colossians 4:1**

Here are some biblical principles for being a good boss:

- *Be a person of integrity.* People need to be able to trust the boss.
- *Make expectations clear.* Take the time to teach, train, and respond to questions.
- *Hold people accountable.* Expecting excellence is good for all.
- *Be fair to all concerned.* Playing favorites is demoralizing to the troops.
- *Lead by building up the team* rather than by leading through intimidation.
- *Genuinely care* about the employee's success as much as your own. This makes your chance for success far greater.
- Remember, you have to answer to God.

God has entrusted authority to you to serve Him and others though leadership. Jesus was the perfect example of servant leadership when He humbled Himself to become one of His own creations and, even more, when He gave His life for those He came to lead.

Jesus is the ultimate CEO, the ultimate boss, the ultimate servant leader.

October 17

ENEMIES IN THE HOME

". . . so that there will not be among you a man or woman,
or family or tribe, whose heart turns away today
from the LORD our God . . ."
—Deuteronomy 29:18

There are many enemies within the home seeking to destroy the family. Let me share a few:

Busyness. Everyone is over-committed, mostly through workaholism and activity-itus. This is true for all ages with our over-organized children's activities.

Lack of spiritual and moral leadership by the father. Approximately thirty-four percent of all births in the U.S. are to single moms. Even in some families that have a dad, he's often absent or practically non-existent.

Negative influence of media and technology. Kids spend more time with the TV than they do with their parents; its influence can be overwhelmingly negative. It's an unfortunate substitute for family communication. Internet pornography is devastating marriages and perverting how some men view women.

Parents, a vibrant relationship with God through Jesus Christ is the best way to battle the many enemies within the home.

October 18

SUFFERING

"For God so loved the world,
that He gave His only begotten Son . . ."
—John 3:16

Do you feel God is distant and remote? That He's unconcerned or doesn't understand your suffering? Many believe the toughest blow in life is to lose a spouse or a child, and it's hard to argue with that.

Have you ever had a child die? God has—His only boy. He understands the pain of a parent when a child dies. Have you ever had a child murdered when they were completely innocent? God has. He understands that type of hatred and rejection.

Could there be a greater evil than to murder an innocent man? No, but this will blow your mind: you are guilty of that evil, and so am I. With our sin, we murdered the Son of God. Amazingly, God in His grace is willing to forgive and give us salvation if we'll simply confess our sin and trust Christ to change us from the inside out.

God understands our suffering, and He's given the greatest thing He could to help us through it. It's called grace.

October 19

Is Heaven All We Hope For?

"The heavens are telling of the glory of God;
and their expanse is declaring the work of His hands."
—Psalms 19:1

Is heaven all we hope for? Dr. R. G. Lee, one of this century's greatest preachers, was in a coma on his deathbed when suddenly his eyes opened. He exclaimed to his daughter, "I see heaven." She said, "Tell me about it." To which Rev. Lee replied, "Oh my sermons never did it justice. I see your mother. I see Jesus. It's so beautiful." Even Dr. Lee couldn't do it justice. Human language is simply inadequate to describe it.

I remember being at the edge of the Grand Canyon, and I stood in awe at the grandeur of the sight. I walk on a quiet beach, and I am in awe of God's creation. But as magnificent as these are, they are nothing compared to heaven.

Imagine being in the presence of the King of the universe and all who follow Him. What a sight that will be! It will be greater than we can hope or imagine. So don't miss out. The ticket for getting there is knowing Jesus Christ as your Savior and Lord.

October 20

OVERCOMING LIFE'S CRISES

"So do not worry about tomorrow,
for tomorrow will care for itself."
—Matthew 6:34

In the fine book, *Men in Midlife Crisis,* Jim Conway uses the Chinese definition of the word crisis. It means opportunity and danger. Life has many crises. How we navigate through these turbulent waters means the difference in a shipwrecked life or a life of victory.

You may be in the middle of a crisis or you may face one in the future. It can be a dangerous time, but also a time for great opportunity. The danger is to panic and make rash decisions with negative long-term consequences. The opportunity is to depend on God for strength. To do this calls for:

- prayer in seeking God's power
- Bible study in seeking God's guidance
- obedience in seeking God's will

Trust God to guide you through the storm.

And one more thing: Take things one day at a time. Jesus said: "Don't be anxious for tomorrow, for tomorrow will take care of itself. Each day has enough trouble of its own."

Are you in a crisis? It's a time of great danger and opportunity. Be aware of the dangers, but don't retreat from the crisis. Become a better person in the process.

REST FOR THE WEARY

"Take My yoke upon you and learn from Me,
for I am gentle and humble in heart,
and YOU WILL FIND REST FOR YOUR SOULS."
—Matthew 11:29

The idea that the pace of life seems to continually increase stress and worry is a universal concept. There seems to be no end to the demands on our time and energy. Are you tired of the rat race?

There is a solution; it isn't one that offers escape from the demands of life, but one that guarantees rest in the midst of the rat race and the fast pace of life. Jesus says, "Come to me if you are tired and burdened. I'll make your load lighter, and help you carry your burden." Jesus offers us rest amidst the stress.

Christ doesn't always take us out of life's demanding situations. Instead, He invites us to allow Him to help us handle the demands. He wants to face each day and each challenge with us. Walking with Jesus Christ daily, and trusting Him for guidance and wisdom to handle whatever comes, is the way to experience rest *in* the rat race.

October 22

Getting Along with Those In-Laws

"Your people shall be my people . . ."
—Ruth 1:16

Perhaps the relationship people struggle with most is getting along with their in-laws. In-laws are the gift we received in marriage, a gift many want to give back.

Even in healthy in-law relationships, there will be tensions and challenges. You both love the same person, and the only reason you're attached is because of that person. That can mean competing interests. In-laws can be made to feel like outlaws. They get to be the brunt of many a tale—especially mothers-in-law, the universal catch-all of abusive humor.

Rather than offer advice on the in-law relationship, I offer four stories in Scripture: For a healthy in-law relationship, read about Moses and his father-in-law in Exodus 18, or Ruth and her mother-in-law in the book of Ruth. If you think you've got it bad, take comfort—it could be a lot worse! Read about Jacob and his father-in-law in Genesis 29 and following, or David and the all time worst in-law, King Saul in 1 Samuel. Hopefully, these will help.

October 23

CREATION OR EVOLUTION

"By faith we understand that the worlds were prepared by the word of God, so that what is seen was not made out of things which are visible."
—Hebrews 11:3

There's a lot of discussion today about creation and evolution. It's important, for understanding our origin is central to understanding who we are, why we're here, and what we're supposed to do on this planet.

Creation is based on the idea that we're here by intelligent design; evolution is based on the idea that we're here by chance. Which makes the most sense? If I were to tell you that your personal computer actually evolved by chance from an explosion in a factory that makes radios, you'd laugh in my face. Yet, is the computer more complex than a human mind? It's amazing that intelligent people know computers are made by intelligent design, yet when it comes to life and earth's design, they choose to believe, "Well, it just evolved by chance." I just don't have enough faith to believe that. Science helps us fill in some of the details of creation, but God is the intelligent designer behind it all.

October 24

THE ULTIMATE MATCHMAKER

". . . for your Father knows what you need before you ask Him."
—Matthew 6:8

There are a lot of matchmakers—relatives, friends, and dating services. TV executives got into the act with their infamous debacle, *Who Wants To Marry A Millionaire?* What a joke! While there have always been matchmakers, finding the right mate is a big decision. What would you want in a matchmaker?

- Someone who knows you and your interests
- Someone who knows the one you're to marry and their interests
- Someone who wants the best for you both—not second best

Good news! There's an ideal matchmaker for everyone. His name is God. He created you. He knows you and your future mate the best, but you have to know Him and seek His best for your life.

If you're single, wouldn't you like to have the perfect matchmaker lead you to the ideal match? Or do you think you know yourself and others better than God does? I think not. Let God be your matchmaker and you won't be disappointed.

MAKING THE MOST OF YOUR TIME

"Therefore be careful how you walk, not as unwise men but as wise, making the most of your time . . ."
—Ephesians 5:15

Do you ever struggle with making the most of your time? Feel there's just not enough time in each day? We have to remember we all have the same amount of time: one hundred sixty-eight hours a week, twenty-four hours a day. The key is making the most of our time. This is a spiritual, as well as practical, issue.

Scripture says, "Be careful, then, how you live, not as unwise men, but as wise, making the most of your time." How do you do that?

List the top three to five priorities in your life. This list will help you prioritize your time.

Concentrate on what's most important, and major on the *majors,* not the minors. As you approach each day, write down the most important thing you need to do; commit to do it, then go to the second most important thing, and do it.

Effective time management is an important discipline for living a successful life; get with it before your time runs out.

October 26

THE SHADOW YOU CAST

"I have put My words in your mouth and have covered you with the shadow of My hand . . . 'You are My people'."
—Isaiah 51:16

In the early days of the church, the Bible tells us in Acts 5 that the apostle Peter had become an influential and powerful man of God. People would bring the sick on pallets and cots to the streets where he might pass. Their hope was that his shadow would fall over them and they would be healed. Such was the aura of greatness around that man.

What kind of shadow do you cast?

Our shadow goes with us wherever we go, never falling on us, but on someone else. We're rarely aware of where it falls. We all influence someone—parents influence kids, coaches influence players, teachers influence students.

What kind of shadow do you cast? Is it for good, or for evil? To build up, or tear down? To encourage, or discourage? To help, or to hurt? Does it point people to God, or just to yourself?

As you think about the life you live, think about the legacy you want to leave. What kind of shadow do you cast?

SIN

"... I say to you, everyone who commits sin is the slave of sin."
—John 8:34

Have you ever noticed that sin has a way of multiplying? The Bible paints a very graphic picture of a person who becomes entrapped by his sin. It says, "And he will be held with cords of his sin." What does that mean?

Have you ever seen a little bug caught in a spider's web? The more that bug struggles to become free, the more entangled it becomes. That's what this verse is talking about. The person is trapped by his sin, and even when he comes to his senses and recognizes the need to change, he cannot escape by his own strength. He just gets more tangled.

But there's hope for the person caught in his sin. We can all be free from bondage by admitting our sin to God and giving Him control of our lives through Jesus Christ. Only He can untangle us from the tangled web of sin we weave!

THE CREATOR REVEALED

"For since the creation of the world His invisible attributes, His eternal power and divine nature, have been clearly seen, being understood through what has been made, so that they are without excuse."
—**Romans 1:20**

I love the fall—the excitement of football season, the crisp coolness of the morning air, the beauty of the changing leaves. This time of year really invigorates me. It's easy to be enthusiastic about life when the world around us is so colorful.

The changing of the seasons reminds us that God created a universe where there is order. Fall follows summer every year. The seasons come like clockwork. So dependable is the change, we take it for granted. The Bible tells us that even if we had no other way of knowing there is a God, nature alone is enough proof of His existence. Creation shows us God's power, and so much of His divine nature.

As you enjoy the change of seasons each year, I hope you'll acknowledge the Creator of such beauty and majesty. He's a God of order in creation and, best of all, His greatest desire is to have a personal relationship with you.

MEETING DEATH

"What man can live and not see death?"
—Psalm 89:48

Peter Marshall used to tell the legend of the merchant of Baghdad who sent his servant to the market in the ancient Middle Eastern city. The servant returned, pale and trembling, and the merchant asked him what was wrong. The servant told him he bumped into someone, looked up, and saw Death in a dark hooded robe pointing at him. He asked the merchant, "Please let me borrow your horse so I can flee to Samara where he can't find me."

The merchant agreed. Later that day, the merchant went to the crowded market and saw Death standing to the side, and he asked, "Why did you frighten my servant?"

Death responded, "I was only shocked to see him in Baghdad, for tonight I have an appointment with him in Samara."

We all have a rendezvous with death. For every life, there is death. The statistics on death are 100 percent. But the fear of death is removed by receiving the promise of eternal life through faith in Jesus Christ. With faith, we can concentrate on living this life to the fullest.

We all have a rendezvous with death. Are you ready?

October 30

WHY DOES GOD ALLOW SUFFERING?

*"For as through the one man's disobedience the many were made
sinners, even so through the obedience of the One the many will
be made righteous."*
—Romans 5:19

A common question is, "How can a loving God allow so much suffering and evil in the world?" It's a tough question that philosophers and theologians have struggled with forever. There is no completely adequate answer, but it's important to remember that God is blamed for a lot of things that man does wrong.

When God created man, He gave us all a free will. He didn't program us as robots to always do what's right or what He wants. Robots have no choice, but humans do. We can choose to trust and obey God—or do things our own way.

From the first man and woman, each person has chosen to go his or her own way rather than God's way. The result of man's sin is disease, suffering, and death.

God did something dramatic to confront the problem: He humbled Himself to become one of us, in the person of Jesus Christ, to show us how to live. Even more, Christ came to die for us. Through faith in Him, we begin to reverse this cycle of evil and suffering.

October 31

Why Prayer Is Disappointing

". . . yet not as I will, but as You will."
—Matthew 26:39

Do you ever feel your prayers are not answered? God's Word gives us the key in James 4:3: "When you ask, you don't receive because you ask with the wrong motives, that you may spend what you get on your pleasures."

The major reason prayer doesn't seem to work is that we tend to pray with selfish motives. God promises to meet our needs, but needs and wants can be two very different things. So much prayer is focused on how we can use God to get what we want. But the greatest example of prayer is found in Jesus. The night before His crucifixion, He asked his Father to spare Him the agony of the cross, but then added, "yet not My will, but Your will."

RACQUETBALL AND LIFE

For this reason we must pay much closer attention to what we have heard, so that we do not drift away from it.

—Hebrews 2:1

A key to success in racquetball is being in the right position on the court. With the ball coming at you from every angle, this sport can make you react like a klutz if you are out of position. Proper positioning can determine a successful reaction; otherwise, watch out for a complete miss!

In life, being out of position makes us unprepared for all the challenges that come our way. God has given us the Bible as our playbook—how to be in the right position as we take on life. God is the ultimate coach for successful living. We can be confident placing our complete trust in His wisdom. When following His playbook to the "T", we will always find ourselves in the proper position to succeed in life. A good player will be prepared, having studied his playbook regularly. Allow God's Word to prepare you for the challenges of life. Get in the game.

Do What's Right

"You shall do what is right and good in the sight of the LORD . . ."
—Deuteronomy 6:18

Society is caught up in the comparison game, and keeping up with the Joneses seems to be the goal of many. Children compare clothes and curfews. Adults compare cars, vacations, and promotions while smiling and patting each other on the back.

Work and moral ethics may be compromised because "my boss does it" or "the guy at church does it." But you and I both know that doesn't make it right. Too many times we justify our actions because we are comparing ourselves by the wrong measure. God's Word gives us the proper standard; all else will fall short of the goal.

Sometimes life requires us to stand up and be counted. Sometimes we must choose between immediate gratification or denying self. Sometimes we simply must go against the grain, because our goal is to please God—not man, or even ourselves. In the long run, we will be better people and will be blessed for it. Do what's right.

Terrible Times in the Last Days

"For men will be lovers of self . . . rather than lovers of God . . ."
—2 Timothy 3:2, 4

Imagine a time in history when "people will be lovers of themselves, lovers of money, arrogant, abusive, disobedient to their parents, ungrateful, unloving, slanderous, without self-control, lovers of pleasure rather than lovers of God; holding to a form of godliness but denying its power." Doesn't this sound like today's world . . . even describing many inside and outside of today's churches!

When were these words penned? Almost 2,000 years ago . . . in the Word of God. This prediction was prefaced with these haunting words: "But realize this, that in the last days difficult times will come" (2 Timothy 3:1).

Sounds like we're there.

How can we change? God's Word says, "The Scriptures are able to make you wise for salvation through faith in Jesus Christ." So study God's Word. Believe what it says about how to be saved from ungodly character. Live what it says, for we all are running out of time.

November 4

First Basics in Victorious Living

". . . Everyone who thirsts, come to the waters . . ."
—Isaiah 55:1

Great football teams focus on the basics of blocking and tackling, over and over and over. Victorious living focuses on the basics as well. The number one basic discipline for victorious living is regular time alone with God.

The prophet Isaiah says, "Ho, everyone who thirsts. Come to the waters." Ho, meaning whoa or slow down. We tend to be like a bunch of racehorses, charging out of the starting gates, rushing into the day without a thought for God. Ho! Slow down and thirst for God. Charging out to make money doesn't satisfy; it leaves your soul empty. God is the source of satisfaction and fulfillment.

Do you have a thirst for God? Ask for a thirst to know Him. Ask God to give you a desire and discipline to spend time with Him, talking and listening to Him through prayer and Bible study. This brings renewal and strength. Regular time alone with God is the first basic in victorious living.

November 5

GOD'S REASONS FOR MARRIAGE

"Then the Lord God said, 'It is not good for the man to be alone; I will make him a helper suitable for him.'"
—Genesis 2:18

Jesus was asked, "Is it lawful for a man to divorce his wife for any reason at all?" He responded by describing what God had in mind for marriage in the first place:

- Marriage is for *procreation*. Jesus said, "He who created man, created man as male and female." God said to Adam and Eve, "Be fruitful and multiply."
- Marriage is also for *companionship*. After God created Adam, He said, "It is not good for man to be alone." So He created Eve, the perfect companion.
- Marriage is also for *sexual pleasure*. As the story continues, Jesus quotes God's words on the first marriage: "and he shall cleave to his wife and the two shall become one flesh." Sex is not just for procreation. It's God's gift to a husband and wife, to enjoy in the context of marriage to the fullest.

Procreation, companionship, sexual pleasure—reminders from Jesus about why God had the idea of marriage.

Noise

"Give ear and hear my voice, listen and hear my words."
—Isaiah 28:23

Have you ever noticed how noise fills our lives? We wake to music or alarms. We get in the car and what's the first thing we do—slip in a tape, CD, or turn on the radio. When we walk into the house or a hotel room, the first thing we do is turn on the TV. It seems that with noise, we just don't feel so alone.

In the midst of all of this noise, are you missing the most important voice of all?

God speaks in a still, small voice. In the busyness and noisiness of our lives, it's easy to miss Him. The only way to hear Him is to make an intentional effort to quiet the noise of our lives and spend some time listening, through prayer and reading His Word. You will never get a more important phone call or crucial message.

Find some time each day to be alone and quiet, and listen to the most important voice of all. It will enrich your life tremendously.

November 7

BIG PROBLEMS WITH THE FIRST

"... Believe in the Lord Jesus, and you will be saved ..."
—Acts 16:31

Let's talk about the big problems of the first family.

No, I'm not referring to the President and the First Lady, but to the original first family, Adam and Eve. They were also the first family to have *big* problems—I mean big problems. Adam and Eve sinned by disobeying God, and their sin infected the whole human race.

They had two boys, Cain and Abel, and the problem of sin carried over to their children's lives. Cain became so jealous of Abel's blessings that he murdered him.

The first family had real problems—from Adam and Eve's simple disobedience, to seeing one of their children murder his brother. The family of man still struggles with the same problem of sin today. But God has a solution in the person of Jesus Christ, who came to save us from our sin problem. When a person looks to Christ, in faith, for salvation from sin, it breaks the negative chain of sin that enslaves people and families.

LIFE SUPPORT

*"For the eyes of the LORD move to and fro throughout
the earth that He may strongly support those
whose heart is completely His."*
—2 Chronicles 16:9

All of us enjoy applause: whether on the athletic field, the stage, the classroom, or in the more insignificant events of life. Every one of us enjoys being praised. Our confidence is bolstered when a person of authority, or anyone we respect, supports us and is on our side. Getting that pat on the back, or that word of encouragement, makes us want to do even better. We work harder. We take on our problems with more determination and vigor. We are infused with *want to.*

Scripture reminds us that God wants to be our cheerleader. The Creator of this universe desires to support us, and support us strongly. He is simply looking for the person who will allow Him to be God. He wants all our heart—all the time—not just when we think we need Him. He is even looking for us. It is not a question of being found by God; He knows exactly where we are. It is a matter of completely giving our heart to Him. With Jesus Christ on our side, we have it all.

WHAT A MAN MOST
NEEDS FROM HIS WIFE

". . . as the church is subject to Christ,
so also the wives ought to be to their husbands in everything."
—Ephesians 5:24

So many wives are clueless about what their husbands need the most. They often make the mistake of thinking his greatest need is like hers—the need for romantic love. But the husband's greatest need is for respect. This is how God has wired him. So, wives, how can you live this out?

Praise him. Build him up, in a world where he often gets beaten down. Just think how much you like to hear the words, "I love you," and praise him just that much and more.

Seek to be his best friend. With his wife, he needs support, not competition. For the most part, men are not as relational and verbal as women.

Have a willingness to follow his lead. You're kidding! In the twenty-first century you want me to follow his lead? Try it. You might just be pleasantly surprised.

If this makes you mad, argue with God, not me. It's from His Book. This is how you really respect your husband. When he senses these things, it's amazing how much he will strive to please *you* and respect what you have to say.

November 10

WHAT A WIFE MOST NEEDS FROM HER HUSBAND

*"Husbands, love your wives,
just as Christ also loved the church . . ."*
—**Ephesians 5:25**

Dr. Dr. James Dobson was asked, "Why are men so insensitive to women's needs today?"

He answered, "I question whether men have really changed all that much. I doubt if men *ever* responded as women preferred. Did the farmer of a century ago come in from the fields to say, 'Tell me how it went with the kids today'? No. He was as oblivious to his wife's nature then as husbands are today."

So men, if you're struggling to meet your wife's needs, the Bible gives a few tips:

- *Physical affection.* Not just sex, but a tender touch which may include a few hugs through the day.
- *Security.* Physical, financial and emotional . . . a wife desires security in all its forms.
- *Understanding.* Listening more than telling her what to do.
- *Reassurance.* Knowing you think she's beautiful, in a society of constant comparison.
- *Spiritual leadership.* Not dictatorship, but servant leadership, like Christ for His church.

These are what a wife needs most from her husband.

November 11

EVIDENCE OF LIFE AFTER LIFE

"Mary Magdalene came, announcing to the disciples,
'I have seen the Lord . . .'"
—John 20:18

All through the ages, man has speculated about life after life. Dante's *Divine Comedy* seeks to describe it. Modern medical science has added to the speculation with its study of near-death experiences. Now all kinds of religions offer their theories.

But the greatest evidence of life after life is in the historical evidence that Jesus rose from the dead. Christianity is the only faith founded by a man who died and came back to life. No other religion makes that claim.

Historical accounts of His appearances to His disciples and over 500 at one time, were written within twenty years of the event. His disciples faced martyrs' deaths for refusing to quit preaching of His death and resurrection.

People don't willingly die for something they know is a hoax. The one thing that would have stopped Christianity in its tracks would have been for Rome or religious authorities to produce the dead body of Jesus. They never did. The best evidence of life after life is the historical evidence of Jesus' resurrection.

Overcoming Fear

"But he who listens to me shall live securely
and will be at ease from the dread of evil."
—Proverbs 1:33

To learn courage, you have to know fear. Isaac Stern, the great violinist, observing a nine-year-old playing the violin amazingly well, said, "You can't really tell how an artist will be until the teen years, for that is when fear comes in. Then and only then can you see if the person has courage. You can't learn courage until you know fear." Fear can paralyze us. Finding the courage to overcome it is a real key to successful living.

One day, Jesus' disciples were caught at sea in a storm. They were afraid they wouldn't make it. Jesus walked out to them and said, "Take courage! It is I. Do not be afraid."

The key to finding courage in the face of fear comes through faith in Jesus Christ. Fear and faith do not mix—they're like oil and water. When faith kicks in, fear moves out, and when faith disappears, fear moves in like a tidal wave. The key to finding the courage to overcome fear is faith.

November 13

Hollywood and a Loss of Reality

"But when He, the Spirit of truth, comes,
He will guide you into all the truth . . ."
—John 16:13

Over the past few years, an interesting development has taken place in the movie world. With movies like *Forrest Gump,* then later with *Contact,* the audience sees scenes that are computer generated. Whether it's Forrest Gump meeting various presidents, or a false interview with President Clinton in *Contact,* they didn't actually occur in life.

After a while, the whole question of truth begins to be greatly blurred, and people wonder whether they can discern the difference between what has actually happened, and what is computer generated. What *is* reality, and what is virtual reality? This increases cynicism in America. We can't trust anything, and we have to doubt everything.

But there is a constant source of truth, and it's found in a person, Jesus Christ. Ultimate truth begins with Him. This truth is revealed in the Bible. It takes faith to believe, but in a world where the truth is increasingly blurred, I urge you to begin with Jesus and His Word, and you will always know the truth.

November 14

A Hand to Hold in the Darkness

"For You light my lamp;
the LORD my God illumines my darkness."
—Psalm 18:28

Why are children afraid of the dark? Maybe it's a fear of being left alone, a feeling of separation, their vivid imagination, or shadows in the dark.

The fact is, children fear the dark for many of the same reasons adults do. It seems many fears intensify in the night—especially sleepless nights. But I have good news: God is with us wherever we go.

Listen to a portion of Psalm 139 (NIV): "Where can I go from your Spirit? Where can I flee from your presence? If I go up to the heavens, you are there; if I make my bed in the depths, you are there. If I rise on the wings of the dawn, if I settle on the far side of the sea, even there your hand will guide me, your right hand will hold me fast."

Like a loving Father, God offers us a hand to hold in life's darkest hours. He'll carry us through the darkness, and lead us where we need to go.

November 15

STARTING POINT FOR BEING A GOOD PARENT

*". . . encourage the young women to love their husbands
[and] to love their children . . ."*
—Titus 2:4

Parenting is an overwhelming calling. We get started with *no* experience, and by the time we *have* experience, it's often too late. So much is out of our control, and there are so many negative influences in our children's lives.

To be a good parent, where should we begin?

The most important starting point is for Mom and Dad to love and respect each other. Why? Because so much of the identity of our children is wrapped up in Mom and Dad. So much of their security is knowing that Mom and Dad really love each other. This means that even if you're divorced, don't make the mistake of tearing down your child by tearing down your ex. Build up your child by portraying your ex in the best possible light, even when it's difficult.

Parenting is tough, but the most important way to be a good parent is to love your spouse. God commands it, and our children need it.

November 16

PARENTING PRESCHOOLERS

"Train up a child in the way he should go,
even when he is old he will not depart from it."
—Proverbs 22:6

This directive from Proverbs gives us great instruction on rearing our children:

- *Train up* means to lead and to teach; teaching your preschooler to obey and to understand who is boss.
- *In the way he should go* means being a student of your child. God has created each of them uniquely, and we want them to discover who God wants them to be.
- *When he is old he will not depart from it.* "Old" doesn't mean teenager or young adult, but aged man.

Along the way, some kids break their parents' hearts, but God's Word offers hope that they will eventually come around. Take time to be a leader and a student of your children when they're small, and there's a far better chance they'll listen to you and do what's right when they're old.

CONVENIENCE BELIEF

"If anyone wishes to come after Me, he must deny himself,
and take up his cross and follow Me."
—Mark 8:34

When I was sixteen, I would have told you I was a Christian. I grew up in a Christian home, but at a Young Life camp in Colorado, I heard a message about God's love for me through Christ's death on the cross. Realizing all He went through convicted me that I believed in God by convenience. I called on God before a big game or a big test, basically using Him.

After realizing God's love for me, I decided to follow Jesus as the number one priority of my life and began a personal relationship with God through Christ.

He loves you just as He loves me. He gave His life so you can know Him personally and be sure of eternal, abundant life with Him. If you just believe in God for convenience, like I used to, consider committing your life to follow Jesus in faith. It's a life you'll never regret. It's a life of ultimate meaning and purpose.

November 18

THE INTERNET

". . . everyone who looks at a woman with lust for her
has already committed adultery with her in his heart."
—Matthew 5:28

In the sense of providing accessible knowledge for all mankind, the Internet has certainly been heralded as one of the greatest tools that has come about since the Guttenberg printing press. Certainly, it is a tremendous tool for doing business and research. But have you thought about one of the problems we face because of the Internet? It is called pornography.

Think about the progression in the last few years; twenty or thirty years ago an adult male who wanted to view hardcore pornography would have to go into an adult theater or bookstore and risk the embarrassment of somebody seeing him. A few years later, video rentals and cable TV made access easier, with less risk of embarrassment. And now with the Internet, hardcore pornography has come into the privacy of the home.

Men and women, listen. Pornography eats away at the core of your intimacy with God and your marriage relationship. It is degrading to women and always harmful to our thoughts and attitudes. It creates an appetite that can never be satisfied. You need to take pro-active steps to avoid the temptations of pornography.

STORMS OF LIFE

"Everyone who hears these words of Mine
and does not act on them,
will be like a foolish man who built his house on the sand."
—Matthew 7:26

Are you ready for the storms of life? Maybe you're currently in a life storm or have recently endured one. One thing's for sure, storms come to us all. The loss of a job, the loss of a spouse, or the words from the doctor, "You've got cancer," are all storms. When we live life, storms come.

Jesus tells a story about two men: One built his house on the sand. The winds and rains came and his house fell in. Another built his house on rock, and when the winds and the rains came, it withstood the storm. The key difference was in the foundation. The greatest foundation for withstanding the storms of life is the rock of Jesus Christ. A close personal relationship with the Lord builds a solid foundation, and that relationship comes through trusting Him and following Him, day by day.

Storms come. Is your foundation secure, built on the rock of Jesus Christ?

The good news is even if you've been blown away by a storm, it's not too late to start rebuilding upon the right foundation.

Appreciation

". . . in everything give thanks;
for this is God's will for you in Christ Jesus."
—1 Thessalonians 5:18

Have you ever given a gift to or done a favor for someone who didn't express appreciation? It's not much fun and certainly doesn't inspire us to give to that person again. If we're honest, we all have to admit that we've failed to say thank you.

Think about the people in service positions we encounter daily. Do you thank the folks at the dry cleaners when your shirts are ready when promised? How about saying thanks to the person behind the counter in the fast-food restaurant? Do you express appreciation to the people in your office who answer the phone or process the mail?

Everyone likes to be appreciated, to hear "thank you" for things they've done well. Why not start today by saying thanks to the people who make your day run so smoothly. While you're at it, thank God for all His blessings in your life.

Saying thank you is always appreciated. It sure makes the day a bit brighter.

GOING HOME

"So he got up and came to his father.
But while he was still a long way off,
his father saw him and felt compassion for him,
and ran and embraced him and kissed him."
—Luke 15:20

Robert Frost wrote, "Home is the place where when you have to go there, they have to take you in." There's no place like home. No matter how bad we mess up or how disappointing life gets, it's the one place they have to take us in.

Jesus told of a wayward son who messed up big time, wasting all his dad had blessed him with. He became homeless and so hungry he wanted to eat leftover slop fit only for animals. But when he came to his senses, he thought about home. He knew he didn't deserve to go there, but he went anyway. And his dad was so overwhelmed with joy he welcomed him home.

The dad represents God, and the wayward son represents you and me. It's Jesus' way of telling us that we all mess up—but nobody messes up so badly that when he decides to come home to the Lord, the Lord won't welcome him back to a right relationship with Him. Is it time for you to come home to the Lord?

Crisis of Grief

"The LORD is near to the brokenhearted
and saves those who are crushed in spirit."
—Psalm 34:18

It isn't a pleasant thought, but at various points in life many of the people we love most are going to die—parents, spouses, friends, siblings, and, sometimes, children. The stats on death are 100 percent. For everyone who lives, death eventually comes. We don't want to think about it, but it's a reality of life.

When it comes, we need to remember there are stages of grief—shock, numbness, denial, anger, depression, and eventually acceptance. In going through the various stages of grief, hold on to these thoughts:

- It's a process; it can't be rushed, but it doesn't last forever.
- With the help of God, it can be a time of growth. If you don't know God, get to know Him.
- Seek the help of others. We all need the support of others to get through it.
- Remember that the first year is the toughest. Don't try to make major decisions right away; give yourself some time.
- If your loved one was a Christian, you can live with the hope that you can see them again. This comes when you also know Christ.

Grief is tough, but with God's help and the help of others, you can make it.

Thanksgiving

"Was no one found who returned to give glory to God . . . ?"
—Luke 17:18

One of life's most common oversights is not taking time to say thanks. We get in such a rush we often forget.

Years ago, ten men with the dreaded disease of leprosy saw Jesus. They were a long distance away, for leprosy was the most feared disease of that day. They were outcasts; people didn't want to touch them for fear of getting the disease. They were treated like many today who have AIDS.

These lepers cried out to Christ to have mercy on them, and He did. He healed them all. What a fantastic day that must have been!

Those ten guys got so excited they all began to run and tell what had happened.

But one turned around and took time to worship and thank Jesus—just one. Jesus asked him, "Weren't there ten? Where are they?" Even God desires to hear thanks.

This week, don't miss a great opportunity to take time to say thanks—to God for His blessings, to friends and loved ones, and to any who helped you along the way.

THE MYTH OF QUALITY TIME

*"You shall teach them diligently to your sons and shall talk
of them when you sit in your house and when you walk
by the way and when you lie down and when you rise up."*
—Deuteronomy 6:7

The May 1997 issue of *Newsweek* had a cover story about the myth of quality time versus quantity time. Ronald Levant, a psychologist at Harvard Medical School, said, "I think quality time is just a way of deluding ourselves into shortchanging our children. Children need vast amounts of parental time and attention. It's an illusion to think that they're going to be on your timetable and that you can say, 'O.K., we've got half an hour, let's get on with it.'" Levant is saying that the idea that quality of time replaces quantity of time that so many boomer parents have bought into, is really a myth.

There *is* no real quality of time unless we have a quantity of time to be with our children during those teachable moments when they're dealing with everyday life. Follow God's will. Invest a quantity of your time with your children, and He'll reward you with a quality relationship that is rich indeed.

God's Family

"That is, it is not the children of the flesh
who are children of God,
but the children of the promise are regarded as descendants."
—Romans 9:8

There are good families and bad families—good ones we're drawn to, and bad ones we want to get away from. No matter what type of family you have, no earthly family lasts forever. They all end in separation through death or man's choice.

But I have good news: There is a family that lasts forever; it begins on earth, and is only realized in perfection after we die. When a person decides to become a follower of Christ, he or she enters a giant family of faith—the church.

There's no perfect church. If you find one, please don't join it. You'll mess it up in a second because we're all sinners who fall short of God's best. But in the family of faith, we're forgiven sinners who begin a process of being transformed into the person God wants us to be. Looking for a family that lasts? Know Jesus and enter into the only family that lasts forever.

Time to Turn on the Light

"I am the Light of the world;
he who follows Me will not walk in the darkness,
but will have the Light of life."
—John 8:12

When you're staying in an unfamiliar place, do you ever awaken in the night and get up without turning on the light? Next thing you know, you're tripping over a suitcase or walking into a table. The last time that happened to me, it was so painful! But when you turn on the light, everything is clear.

A lot of folks are trying to make it through life in darkness—spiritual darkness—and much self-inflicted pain and unnecessary falls take place, because most people in the dark feel they're doing just fine on their own.

But Jesus tells us He's the light of the world. He means He is the enlightenment about God, man, and life. Without Him, we're in the dark spiritually. We keep stumbling, falling, and feeling frustrated about it all. Hey, isn't it time for some of you folks to turn on the light, really see God, and understand life? If you do, everything will make sense.

FACING REJECTION

"As for me, I said in my alarm,
'I am cut off from before Your eyes.'
Nevertheless You heard the voice of my supplications
when I cried to You."
—**Psalm 31:22**

Rejection is a part of life. We all face it, whether trying out for a team and being cut, being fired, or laid off. Toughest of all may be rejection in the family through a divorce, a child feeling rejected by a parent, or one sibling rejecting another.

Remember, God's power is sufficient for you to overcome rejection. How?

1. You have to trust Him completely to bring good out of the worst rejection.
2. You have to confess to God any feelings of resentment, bitterness, or anger and ask God to forgive you. Remember, "Bitterness is the poison we swallow while hoping the other person dies."
3. You have to ask God to give you the power to forgive the person who rejected you, and for the strength to move on.

Jesus is our ultimate example for dealing with rejection. He chose to forgive on the cross, and He gives us the power to do the same when others reject us.

CONTENTMENT

"Not that I speak from want,
for I have learned to be content in whatever circumstances I am."
—Philippians 4:11

One of the most rare commodities in society is contentment. Advertisers would have us believe that their product is the key to finding fulfillment and happiness. Television programming reinforces this message and fills our homes with images of things. It's like this "stuff" is essential to our happiness.

Seeking satisfaction in things will never bring contentment; it just leads to further dissatisfaction. How do we find contentment? Like so many other things, contentment is a choice—a by-product.

A man who had more than his share of difficulty in life said, "I have learned to be content regardless of my circumstances." It was the apostle Paul who said that. How did he do it? The key was found in his relationship with Jesus Christ. That's the key for anyone. We all have the same opportunity to find contentment. It's a by-product of our relationship with Jesus Christ, our Savior and Lord. That is the key to being content.

GRIEF

"Therefore, you have grief now; but I will see you again,
and your heart will rejoice,
and no one will take your joy away from you."
—John 16:22

Losing a loved one or a close friend is never easy, but understanding the stages of grief can sometimes help. Grief involves numbness and denial, promoting an inability to feel when the news of a death arrives, and a sense of disbelief that the person is really gone. It involves tearful emotion as the reality of a permanent separation sets in.

The loss of the loved one can involve anger at God or life as the world continues on when you're hurting so bad. It can involve depression, or feeling that life is meaningless. Finally, there is acceptance—coming to terms with the loss, and beginning to move on with life.

The grieving process takes time, but it can be overcome. The greatest strength for getting through it is found in the Lord. Remember, God understands your grief. He knows what it's like to have a child die. He saw His own son, Jesus, die for us all. He loves you and wants to help you overcome your grief if you'll let Him.

Bringing Good Out
of a Bad Situation, Part 1

*". . . the sufferings of this present time are not worthy to be
compared with the glory that is to be revealed to us."*
—Romans 8:18

In your mind, picture a fifty-two-year-old executive, writer, artist, and speaker who has a national radio broadcast. What would you think if I told you that same person has been a quadriplegic since she was seventeen? Some of you know her name—Joni Erikson Tada. Her life has been an inspiration to many because she believes God can bring good out of the worst situation. She believes that suffering has purpose through faith in God, for God can use suffering to mold our character to make us a better person.

Are you going through a difficult time? Does your hardship and suffering seem meaningless?

Remember, God can take the worst life brings and turn it into something good if you'll put your trust in Him. He's in the business of turning chaos into a masterpiece when we turn our life over to Him.

Are you willing to believe God can bring good out of your situation? I assure you He can.

December 1

BRINGING GOOD OUT OF A BAD SITUATION, PART 2

". . . we toil, working with our own hands; when we are reviled,
we bless; when we are persecuted, we endure . . ."
—1 Corinthians 4:12

In March 1999, a twenty-three-year-old man named Steve Sawyer died of AIDS. Most of you wouldn't know the name, but he shared his story with over 100,000 college students.

He was a hemophiliac, and in the 1980's he contracted the HIV virus through a blood transfusion. For years he was bitter. What could be more unfair? But he accepted Christ as his Savior and Lord in college, and when AIDS took over he realized he had only a short time to live. Steve wanted to tell as many as possible that, through Christ, he had found peace and ultimate victory. He said, "This is what God has given me to do: my calling was to have AIDS, and share the gospel through AIDS."

Amazing! If you were suffering like him, could you say that? It's the power of the Gospel to bring good out of bad situations. After all, AIDS killed Steve, but Christ overcame death; and now, so has Steve Sawyer.

December 2

WHAT IS THE GOSPEL?

*"To give His people the knowledge of salvation
by the forgiveness of their sins . . ."*
—**Luke 1:77**

If you're not a Christian but you've been around Christians, you've probably heard the term "gospel," but what does it mean?

It means God loves you. He has a purpose for your life. He wants you to have a meaningful life. That's the great part! Everybody likes that.

But we have a problem personally experiencing God's love. We're separated from God because of our sin. Sin is missing the mark of God's best for our life. It's living life *our* way versus *God's* way. But the solution is Jesus. He died for our sins. He rose from the dead, proving He is God. He is the way to God.

This calls for a decision to believe Jesus is who He says He is, and to trust Christ alone for salvation and abundant life.

That's it. Do you believe it? The Gospel is the good news of salvation, following the bad news of our sin problem. I hope you'll believe it *and* receive it.

December 3

CHILDLIKE FAITH

"... Let the children alone, and do not hinder them from
coming to Me; the kingdom of heaven belongs to such as these."
—**Matthew 19:14**

Parents pushed and shoved their children, hoping the famous man would touch them. His assistants, thinking they were protecting Him from unwanted demands, tried to shoo the kids away, but this important man was indignant with His assistants. He said, "Let the children come to Me." He took them in His arms and hugged them, and the kids loved Him. The man's name was Jesus. He showed His well-intentioned disciples how important children are to God.

Question: Dad . . . Mom . . . do you make time for your kids like Jesus did? The man who lived an incredibly busy life was not too busy for children.

Very often, a child's importance is shown when we give a listening ear or a hug, when time is what they want and need. When it comes to your kids, ask the Lord to help you be like Jesus. No job is more important than that; even if you're the Son of God.

December 4

REAL VS. COUNTERFEIT

"And many false prophets will arise, and will mislead many."
—**Matthew 24:11**

The U.S. Treasury Department is charged with keeping our monetary supply free from counterfeit bills. Do you know how Treasury agents are trained to recognize counterfeit currency? They spend hours studying the real thing—the real notes. They become so familiar with true currency, that false ones are easily recognized.

The same principle applies in the spiritual realm. All around us are belief systems that promise to discover the God within you, or the ability to delve into psychic mysteries, or those that assure that we have innate goodness and the need for no authority beyond ourselves.

These counterfeit beliefs seek to turn our attention from the true God revealed in Jesus Christ. You can avoid being trapped by a lie. However, if you'll spend time getting to know Christ and His teachings in Scripture, false ideas are easily seen, because in comparison to knowing Christ, other ideas don't even come close.

Do you know the real thing?

December 5

PATIENCE

"He who is slow to anger has great understanding,
but he who is quick-tempered exalts folly."
—Proverbs 14:29

It has been said that life is a test of patience. Where do you struggle with being patient?

I struggle with lines—whether it's traffic, or waiting at a restaurant. Why, I'd rather drive five miles out of the way than sit still in traffic. I get impatient with people when I'm facing a deadline and get interrupted, or when someone says they'll do something and it doesn't get done.

Where do you struggle with patience? Do you ever pray, "Lord, give me some patience, now!" Let me suggest a few practical ways to learn patience:

1. Take a breath, and pray for self-control.
2. When people anger you, if possible, retreat for a moment. Take time to back off and get control of your emotions.
3. Confront fairly, and seek to listen, understand, and where needed, forgive.
4. Remember, the greatest motive for patience is remembering God's patience with us.

Patience is a precious commodity, for it's a powerful way to win the respect of others and turn a potential enemy into a friend.

December 6

THE PERFECT WISH

*"So give Your servant an understanding heart to judge
Your people to discern between good and evil."*
—1 Kings 3:9

As kids we used to play a game asking that question, "If you could make one wish, what would it be?"

I would stay quiet while others said things like, lots of money, a big house, or a motorcycle. Then I'd say, "I'd wish for unlimited wishes!" I felt so smart, but looking back it simply revealed incredible selfishness.

Years ago God said to Israel's young King Solomon, "Ask whatever you wish Me to give you." What an offer! Solomon chose "wisdom to lead and discernment between good and evil." God was pleased, knowing he could have asked for wealth or a long life. So God granted his wish *and* a wealthy, long life.

Asking God for wisdom is a wise request indeed, for so often with wisdom comes great success and the respect of others. The world is drawn to people who are wise. Remember, God and His Word are the best sources of wisdom.

December 7

COURAGE

"Be on the alert, stand firm in the faith,
act like men, be strong."
—1 Corinthians 16:13

It has always fascinated me to read the accounts of the Allied invasion at Normandy. It was a day of overwhelming tragedy and innumerable acts of courage. Hearing the accounts of bravery performed on the beaches by those men who distinguished themselves fighting for freedom brings awe to all.

But acts of courage don't occur only on the battlefield. Courageous deeds happen unnoticed on playgrounds, in offices, and in homes every day as people stand up for what's right. Courage is understanding the consequences, and choosing to do the right thing anyway.

About 2,000 years ago a man named Jesus Christ, a man who had never sinned, chose to go to the cross for your sins and mine. It was the ultimate act of courage. And His sacrifice, like the men at Normandy, was done for you. When you finally recognize what His sacrifice means, I encourage you to choose to trust Him. He will then give you courage to face every day victoriously.

December 8

INNER BEAUTY VS. OUTER BEAUTY

"Your adornment must not be merely external . . .
but let it be the hidden person of the heart . . ."
—1 Peter 3:3–4

The world puts a lot of focus on women's beauty: makeup, jewelry, clothing, and of course, the right hairstyle. And don't forget taking care of her body! Certainly, men are drawn to beauty in a woman, and women know beauty is power.

But God's Word says something interesting to women: "Let not your adornment be merely external—but let it be the hidden person of the heart." God's Word is reminding every woman that outward beauty is temporal, but inner beauty from godly character and spirit is imperishable. Think about older ladies whose countenance becomes more beautiful with age.

God isn't saying, "Don't be concerned about making the most of your appearance." You should, for I assure you, the man in your life wants you to be. But God wants women to remember the only type of beauty that lasts. He wants you to focus, most of all, on godly beauty that gives a woman lasting splendor that grows greater with age.

December 9

THE HUMBLING POWER
OF GOD AT CHRISTMAS

". . . [Jesus] humbled Himself by becoming obedient to the point
of death, even death on a cross . . . God highly exalted Him,
and bestowed on Him the name which is above every name . . ."
—Philippians 2:8–9

A few years ago, a famous designer by the name of Versace was mur-dered in Miami. Andrea Lee was quoted as having asked Versace earlier if he believed in God, and this is what he said: "Yes, I believe in God but I'm not the kind of religious person who goes to church, who believes in the fairy tale of Jesus born in the stable with the donkey. That . . . no, I'm not that stupid. I can't believe in that God with all the power that He has, that He had to have Himself born in a stable. It would have been too uncomfortable."

Here was a hero of contemporary culture who said he believed in God, but didn't need all that "Jesus" stuff. But the wonder of the Christmas story is that God, with all His power, humbled Himself to become a man and, even more, to die for us—to be our Savior. There was certainly no degree of comfort in that. God did this because He loves you and me, and that's a God worth believing.

THE INTRUSION OF JESUS

"... WHOEVER WILL CALL ON THE NAME
OF THE LORD WILL BE SAVED."
—**Romans 10:13**

Despite man's efforts to eliminate Christ from of Christmas . . . out of everyday life . . . out of government . . . out of schools . . . out of the marketplace—He just won't go away.

Peter Larson writes, "Despite our efforts to keep Him out, God intrudes. The life of Jesus is bracketed by two impossibilities: a virgin's womb and an empty tomb. Jesus entered our world through a door marked 'No Entrance' and left through a door marked 'No Exit.'"

That first Christmas, there was no room for Him in the inn. The world never wants to make room for Christ at Christmas and in everyday life. Man killed Him and sealed the tomb with a huge stone to shut Him out of our lives once and for all. But God removed the stone to prove Jesus will not be shut up or shut out of His plans.

One day Jesus will intrude on history again. The way to be ready is to invite Him into your life today. Will you shut Him out, or let Him in.

December 11

ONE MAN'S SIN: LONG-TERM CONSEQUENCES

*"For I know that nothing good dwells in me, that is, in my flesh;
for the willing is present in me, but the doing of the good is not."*
—Romans 7:18

Very often, we rationalize sin by thinking nobody will be hurt . . . it's no big deal. But sin has a way of having lasting consequences. Do you know the origin of the Middle East conflict? It goes back to the sin of one man, Abraham, the father of three faiths: Judaism, Christianity, and Islam.

God promised to bless Abraham and his wife, Sarah, with a son He would use to build a great nation. Because they were very old, Sarah suggested to Abraham that he sleep with her younger maidservant, and have their child through her. This was a legally acceptable solution, but it wasn't in God's will. The servant gave birth to Abraham's first son, Ishmael. Abraham's wife became resentful, and the maidservant and Ishmael fled to the desert.

But God eventually gave Abraham and Sarah the son He promised—Isaac. From Isaac came the Jews and Israel; from Ishmael came the Arabs. The descendants of these two sons of Abraham have been in conflict ever since. One man's sin—long-term consequences. So let's trust God and do right.

December 12

THE CREATOR AND HIS CREATURES

"I WILL BE A FATHER TO HIM
AND HE SHALL BE A SON TO ME..."
—Hebrews 1:5

One day a bird, caught in our chimney, flew into our house. We tried desperately to get it out the door, but it didn't get the message. After a while, totally frustrated, I had the ridiculous thought, "If I could become a bird for a few seconds and talk its language, I could show it how to be free." Then I remembered that God did just that.

The Creator of the universe became one of His own creatures—a man—to communicate perfectly with mankind. Jesus took on a human body and personality, with all its limitations, so you and I could understand how to be free to live and have a relationship with God.

This is really what Christmas is all about. God chose to reveal Himself to us in the form of a baby, Jesus Christ. When we get to know the God who loves us so much that He would humble Himself to become a man, then Christmas always has a sense of wonder.

December 13

TIME

"... [the Lord] has saved us and called us with a holy calling,
not according to our works, but according to His own purpose
and grace which was granted us
in Christ Jesus from all eternity."
—2 Timothy 1:9

Do you hear the clock ticking? Time keeps moving on. It never stops for anyone—no matter how important you are. We just can't find enough of that stuff. The late Jim Croce sang about bottling time. But one thing's for sure—God wants us to be good stewards of our time, but we'll never be able to until we're clear about our purpose for living. The starting point is knowing why we're here.

First, ask God to help you develop a life-purpose statement. It will take some time, but it's the best time you'll ever invest. Know why you're here. Second, decide each day what's most important for you to do that day, and do it. By having a clear purpose, and doing the most important thing each day, God can revolutionize your life and help you make the most of your time.

December 14

Supernatural Birth

*"... an angel of the Lord appeared to him in a dream, saying,
'Joseph, son of David, do not be afraid to take Mary as your
wife; for the Child who has been conceived in her
is of the Holy Spirit.'"*
—Matthew 1:20

Imagine your high school honey, whom you love and believe is a good person because she doesn't believe in sex before marriage, saying, "I'm pregnant, but don't be mad, because I'm still a virgin." How would you respond?

This scenario really happened about 2,000 years ago. In fact, the guy was named Joe, and his pregnant girlfriend was Mary. She told him God caused her to become pregnant.

At first, Joe didn't believe Mary, and thought about breaking up with her. When an angel appeared to Joe and told him Mary was telling the truth, he stayed with her, believing the Lord in faith.

For the rational, secular, scientific mind of the twenty-first century, this story is incredible. But it's the story of Christmas—the story of Jesus' birth. The question: Do you believe? Be it Jesus' birth or His resurrection, I want you to know you've got to believe it fully to experience the wonder of Christmas.

December 15

MARY—A GREAT EXAMPLE OF FAITH

"But Mary treasured all these things,
pondering them in her heart."
—Luke 2:19

The Bible could never be accused of whitewashing the heroes of the faith. Abraham, Jacob, Moses, David, and Peter all had some pretty serious flaws and failures. When we come across a biblical personality who had no recorded obvious flaws and sins, we take note. Mary, the mother of Jesus, is one of those who was always found faithful. And what faith she had! She was a Jewish teenage virgin visited by an angel, and told she would give birth to God's son.

I love Mary's realness. She initially responded like any teenage virgin would today. Disbelief, shock, bewilderment—probably wondering what her fiancé and her family would think. She asked, "How can this be since I am a virgin?" But after the initial shock, she chose to believe God's Word. She's the first to believe in Jesus as her Savior and Lord—while she carried Him in her womb.

She's the true first lady of the faith. Do you believe as Mary did? What God's Word says about Jesus is true.

THE INCOMPARABLE CHRIST

*". . . All authority has been given to Me
in heaven and on earth."*
—Matthew 28:18

No person has had more impact on history than Jesus Christ. It is undeniable that He lived and walked in the land of Judea and Israel almost 2,000 years ago. But who is He?

- He is the visible image of the invisible God. *He is God in a person. You want to know what God is like? Look to Jesus. The fullness of God dwells in Him.*
- He is also the Creator of all creation. *He holds all creation together. It is His masterpiece. Creation reveals the greatness of God.*
- He is the Savior who saves us from our sins. *He came to reconcile us with God.*
- He is the head of the church. *He is to the church what the head is to the body.*

Once you know who He is, you have a choice—a decision to make. It's the biggest one ever—to trust Him as your Savior and Lord or to reject Him. Who is Jesus? The Bible is clear, but the important thing for you is, do you believe it?

SEEKERS

"Where is He who has been born King of the Jews?"
—Matthew 2:2

There are all sorts of seekers today, searching for truth and the answer to life. Would you describe yourself as a seeker? The original seekers were three guys from the east. They weren't Christian or Jewish, but were searching for meaning.

God spoke to them through the heavens with the appearance of a new star. They stepped out on faith, believing that what they were seeing signified the birth of a new king. Along the way, God spoke to them through Scripture, prophesizing the Messiah would be born in Bethlehem. They stepped out on faith and went there, seeking.

When they arrived, they found the answer to life in a little boy named Jesus. They believed He was God who had become a man . . . and our Savior. They found what every seeker needs . . . Jesus . . . the answer to life. Today, wise men still seek Him.

Birth Announcement

". . . you shall call His name Jesus,
for He will save His people from their sins."
—Matthew 1:21

One type of letter we often get in our household is a birth announcement—someone announcing the birth of a child—a wonderful time of celebration and excitement. But when Jesus Christ was born, the ultimate birth announcement came straight from heaven when God, through His angels, said, "Today in the city of David has been born for you a savior who is Christ the Lord."

You may ask, "Why do I need a savior?"

God's Word is clear that we need a savior because all of us sin, and in the process, find ourselves separated from God. If we die separated, that means hell . . . and that's bad news. But Christmas is about good news, because Christ came to pay the penalty for our sins so we could be forgiven and made right with God. For those who believe, He saves us from sin and, ultimately, hell . . . and that's pretty important.

As you rush around getting ready for Christmas, remember why He came and believe it. That's the key to having a Merry Christmas.

December 19

PLAYING GOD

"The way of a fool is right in his own eyes . . ."
—Proverbs 12:15

Dr. Jack Kevorkian has belittled the medical profession, those who are religious, the government, the courts, and the press. He once said, "Pass any law you want—I don't care. I know what's right. I'm going to do what's right."

Dr. Kevorkian was then asked, "Is there no higher authority on earth to which you will submit?"

He replied, "Oh, well, I don't know of one."

I sat there stunned. A man who submits to no authority but himself is a dangerous man. The man who most comes to mind with that kind of mindset was Adolf Hitler. He, too, decided there was no higher authority to submit to, and certain lives were not worth living—say, about six million Jews!

Even more shocking was the statistic that seventy-three percent of the American public agreed with what Dr. Kevorkian was doing. That means the overwhelming majority feels it's OK to play God. When man decides to do that, man soon justifies almost any evil in a self-righteous way.

America . . . wake up! We are called to trust God, not play God. For when we play God, we act like the Devil. And that's bad for us all.

December 20

Belief in the Virgin Birth

". . . Behold, a virgin will be with child and bear a son,
and she will call His name Immanuel."
—Isaiah 7:14

Christmas is about a virgin birth. Do you believe it? Think about what it means if it isn't true:

1. It means Joseph and Mary lied about Jesus' birth, which makes them despicable or delusional.
2. It means the Bible contains lies, which makes it an untrustworthy book.
3. It means the true nature of Jesus is missed—for without it, He's just a man, conceived like you and me.

Question: Do you believe Jesus rose from the dead?

The Bible is clear. A person can't be a Christian if he doesn't believe it. Yet some so-called enlightened Christians believe in Jesus' resurrection, but not His virgin birth. Often motivated by a desire to have fire insurance and yet be sophisticated, their intellectual inconsistency of believing one miracle and not another is a wonder to behold. If Jesus rose from the dead, what's the big deal about His virgin birth?

With God, nothing is impossible. I believe it's true because I believe the Bible is trustworthy. What about you?

Christmas, without the virgin birth, is just an empty shell.

Alone, But Not Lonely

". . . I am with you always, even to the end of the age."
—Matthew 28:20

Some feel it in a crowd; others feel it when alone. Sociologists say that never before in history have so many people lived so close together and felt so far apart. Loneliness is a major problem. There's no doubt that singles bars are filled with people battling loneliness. A divorced person, tired of one-night stands, recently said, "Sex is readily available in the American singles scenes, but friendship is not."

I propose to you that one can still be alone but not lonely. A person will never find victory over loneliness until he learns to enjoy being alone. At the root of all loneliness is alienation from God.

Years ago, a man named Augustine espoused that God has made us for Himself. Our soul is restless until we find rest in Him. We may seek to fill the void with activities, crowds, and noise, but a nagging loneliness will always be there until we have a personal relationship with God. When we find that, we have found the key to being alone, but not lonely.

Folks Who Missed Christmas

". . . seeing they do not see, and while hearing they do not hear,
nor do they understand."
—Matthew 13:13

Christmas comes—Christmas goes—but there are always many who miss out on the real meaning of Christmas. It's always been that way, and the first Christmas reminds us of those who missed Christmas:

1. The innkeeper. He was so busy—a full hotel and so many customer needs. No time or place in his inn for Jesus at Christmas.
2. Religious leaders around King Herod. When the wise men came inquiring about the birth of a kingly Messiah, the religious leaders told Herod that God's Word said Bethlehem. Yet, they were so focused on staying close to worldly power they didn't take God's Word seriously. They missed Jesus at Christmas.
3. Herod. He tried to eliminate Christmas before it got off the ground, to eradicate Jesus from Christmas. People are still seeking to use political power to do that today.

Will you miss Christmas as well? If you find Jesus in all the commotion, you will not ever miss Christmas again.

December 23

Folks Who Found Christmas

". . . he who comes to God must believe that He is and
that He is a rewarder of those who seek Him."
—Hebrews 11:6

It's easy to miss the real meaning of Christmas, but the story of Christmas tells us who found it:

1. The shepherds. They were social nobodies, yet God sent them a supernatural birth announcement through the angels. They believed God's Word, searched in faith to find Jesus, and they did. They found Christmas.
2. The wise men. These guys were pagans from another culture. They studied the stars for insight. But God spoke to them right where they were in life. They stepped out in faith to follow a star that appeared in the sky, understanding it meant the birth of a special King. They found Christmas when they found Jesus.

The shepherds found Christmas because they believed the Word of God. The wise men found Christmas because, as seekers, they found Jesus. Find Jesus as Savior and Lord, and you'll find Christmas—guaranteed!

December 24

GIVING AT CHRISTMAS

". . . they fell to the ground and worshipped Him. Then, opening
their treasures, they presented to Him gifts of
gold, frankincense, and myrrh."
—**Matthew 2:11**

Giving and Christmas go hand in hand; but have you ever thought about where giving gifts at Christmas originated? Some will suggest giving began with St. Nicholas, commonly known as Santa Claus; but it was long before St. Nick.

It began with some men who visited Jesus when He was a young child. They became known as the three wise men. They brought gifts of gold, frankincense, and myrrh.

Gold is the gift for a king, an expensive gift symbolizing belief that Jesus was born to be a king. Frankincense is the gift for a priest, reminding us that Jesus is the ultimate High Priest, a mediator between God and man. But myrrh was an unusual gift for a child. It's a precious spice or perfume used to anoint a body at death. Why myrrh? It was a prophetic gift. Jesus had come to die to be our Savior—to give His life for our sins.

King. Priest. Savior. Three gifts which reveal to us, at Christmas, who Jesus is.

December 25

VISITED BY AN ANGEL

". . . the angel said to them, 'Do not be afraid; for behold,
I bring you good news of great joy which will be
for all the people . . .'"
—**Luke 2:10**

Have you ever been visited by an angel? A popular TV series was built around people who were "touched by an angel" and usually weren't aware of it. But say you're a security guard on the late night shift patrolling a business and suddenly an angel appears before you, hovering in the sky. You know right away it's an angel, and you're so scared you can't move, yell for help, or grab your gun—you're just scared speechless. Then the angel speaks and says, "Easy, don't be afraid. I've got good news to share. A Savior has been born and God wants you to be the first to know."

Pretty wild, eh? But this same type of scenario happened about 2,000 years ago to some shepherds on their watch one night in the hills of Bethlehem. It must have been something! More importantly, they believed the angel. They went to worship Jesus that first Christmas. You can, too, when you seek Jesus in Scripture and believe.

December 26

THE DEATH OF COMMUNISM

"TODAY IF YOU HEAR HIS VOICE,
DO NOT HARDEN YOUR HEARTS."
—Hebrews 4:7

I'll never forget Christmas Day 1991. It's not a special family memory, but a great day in history. The world watched as the Soviet Union's leader resigned and the Communist red hammer and sickle flag was lowered for the last time.

Isn't it interesting that the very government which tried to destroy Christianity for more than seventy years officially ended on Christmas Day? God's sense of timing is perfect. He must have chuckled on that Christmas. Isn't that amazing?

My friends, God is in control of all of history. His plans are sure. His timing is perfect—from the birth of His Son, to the end of the Soviet Union on Christmas Day. And one day, in His perfect timing, Jesus will return. The way history is moving, it won't be long. Let us all be ready for His coming by walking in God's will every day, through faith in Christ.

Suicide—An Option?

". . . choose life . . . by loving the LORD your God,
by obeying His voice, and by holding fast to Him."
—Deuteronomy 30:19–20

Through the years, we've heard in the news about Dr. Jack Kevorkian, the doctor of death (if that isn't an oxymoron!) who chose to make assisted suicide his cause. His actions elicit strong emotions, because no one wants to see a loved one suffer, and no one desires to endure long-term pain and disability. But it really comes down to a question of faith.

Long ago, a man named Job suffered incredible loss—all his possessions and his children—and had to endure an agonizing illness. If anyone had a right to end his life, it was Job. And yet, Job chose to put his trust in God. He asked, "Will I accept the good things God gives and refuse the bad?"

This is a question we should all consider. Is freedom from pain my right as a human being? Is life only worth living if everything is going my way? In the face of eternity, trusting a loving and sovereign God is really the best choice. Only God has the right to give and take life.

THE BASICS OF MONEY MANAGEMENT

"For where your treasure is, there your heart will be also."
—Luke 12:34

Let's talk about the basics of successful money management. Jesus says we have to choose where we put our trust. He says we have to choose between God and money.

God helps us master our money, rather than letting money master us, and He does it through these principles:

- *Spend less than you earn.* Know where you stand with what you have and where you spend it.
- *Develop a budget plan.* A good budget has five key considerations:

  1. *Giving to God.* Begin here. Giving first shows you trust Him, and not money.
  2. *Savings and investments.* This helps with short-term surprises and long-term needs.
  3. *Taxes.* God's Word tells us to pay what we owe.
  4. *Fixed expenses.* This includes things like mortgage, utilities, cars, etc.
  5. *Discretionary spending.* This includes entertainment, clothes, furniture, etc.

God's ways for basic money management . . . they work.

December 29

GOD'S CREATION

"God saw all that He had made, and behold, it was very good."
—Genesis 1:31

Isn't God's creation a wonder to behold? I'm always amazed when I watch the Discovery Channel or a *National Geographic* special on an in-depth study of an animal I've rarely seen, gaining insight about what makes them unique and how they survive.

Even though God is rarely—if ever—mentioned on these shows, it causes my faith to soar, for I'm reminded that God thought of everything, every little detail in creating this living thing. Everywhere you turn in creation, there's evidence of intelligent design—the work of the Master Artist.

Let me ask you something: When you see a great painting . . . Da Vinci's *Mona Lisa*, a piece by Van Gogh, or a scene of American life by Norman Rockwell, do you have more awe of the piece of art than of the artist? Not likely. Yet we do this all the time with God's creation. If we honor the creation and forsake the Creator, we miss everything. The best way to appreciate creation is to know and appreciate the Creator.

THE LAST DAY

". . . godliness is profitable for all things,
since it holds promise for the present life
and also for the life to come."
—1 Timothy 4:8

If you received an official notice today that this is your last day to live, what would you do? Would you try to make more money, or stay late at the office working hard? Would you spend time with your family, or express thanks to those who've helped you along the way? Would you seek to get right with God?

We tend to focus on the material and the temporal and neglect the eternal and relational. But none of us knows the number of days God has planned for us. Don't put off until tomorrow the really important things you can do today—like getting right with God. God became a man in the person of Jesus to show us how. Start there, and show your family how much you love them. Surprise them by occasionally coming home early. Tell them you love them. Plan fun things to do with them. Help someone you care about—someone who needs you at the office, in the neighborhood, or maybe someone who needs a friend.

It may not be the last day you live on earth, but it may become a great day for you and those you care about.

*. . . keep them in Your name, the name which You have given
Me, that they may be one even as We are.*
—John 17:11

Redeemer   Son of Man   King of Kings   The Rock

I AM   The Way   The Truth   The Life

Lion of Judah   The Hope of Glory   Ancient of Days

Lord   Son of God   Lord of Lords   The Christ

God With Us   Immanuel

Savior   **JESUS**   The Word

Wonderful Counselor   Everlasting Father

Prince of Peace   Fully God—Fully Man   Messiah   Lamb of God

Advocate   Alpha   Omega   Bread of Life

Chief Cornerstone   Good Shepherd   Great High Priest

Deliverer   Morning Star   Resurrection   Almighty God

JUST ONE MORE MINUTE . . .

There are a lot of minutes in the day. There are really a lot of minutes in a month, in a year, and in a lifetime. But have you ever thought about how many minutes are in an eternity? Your earthly life will expire some day, and you will spend eternity—that's forever and ever—either in heaven or in hell. Heaven is forever in the presence of God; hell is truly a living hell of torment, eternally separated from God. But now, in the very next minute, you can determine where you spend that eternity. It really is that simple, but it is indeed a profound minute. The decision must be heartfelt. It must be genuine. This next minute truly can change your life forever—but the choice is absolutely and completely yours.

Consider the following questions:

1. *Can you admit you really do need God and are separated from Him by your sinfulness?*

   For all have sinned and fall short of the glory of God
   —Romans 3:23

2. *Are you willing to turn from your selfish ways and yield your heart to God?*

   If we confess our sins, He is faithful and just to forgive us and to cleanse us from all unrighteousness
   —1 John 1:9

3. *Will you believe, with a heart of faith, that Christ died for you and then rose again from death itself?*

    For the wages of sin is death, but the free gift of God is eternal life in Christ Jesus our Lord
    —**Romans 6:23**

    For Christ died for our sins according to the scriptures, and He was buried, and He was raised on the third day according to the scriptures
    —**1 Corinthians 15:3–4**

4. *What is holding you back? The choice is totally yours. Eternity cannot be earned or inherited. You must personally invite Jesus Christ into your life, willingly and openly, and trust the Holy Spirit to fill your heart with this gift of grace.*

    Behold, I stand at the door and knock; if anyone hears My voice and opens the door, I will come in to him and will dine with him and he with Me
    —**Revelation 3:20**

A SIMPLE PRAYER
THAT CAN CHANGE YOUR LIFE . . .

Dear Lord Jesus,

    I know I continue to fall short, and need Your forgiveness. I believe You died for my sins. I want to turn from my sins and give You control of my life. I now invite You to come into my heart and life. I want to follow You and trust You as my personal Lord and Savior. Thank You for Your grace and forgiveness in my life.

    I pray in the powerful name of Jesus, amen.

_____

Signature

_____

Date

To order additional copies of

ONE MINUTE
OF YOUR
Day

Have your credit card ready and call

Toll free: (877) 421-READ (7323)

or order online at: www.winepressbooks.com